EDUCATION FOR SUSTAINABLE DEVELOPMENT IN THE CARIBBEAN

EDUCATION FOR SUSTAINABLE DEVELOPMENT IN THE CARIBBEAN

PEDAGOGY, PROCESSES AND PRACTICES

LORNA DOWN AND THERESE FERGUSON

The University of the West Indies Press

Jamaica • Barbados • Trinidad and Tobago

The University of the West Indies Press
7A Gibraltar Hall Road, Mona
Kingston 7, Jamaica
www.uwipress.com

A catalogue record of this book is available from the National Library of
Jamaica.

ISBN: 978-976-640-890-9 (print)
978-976-640-892-3 (ePub)

Cover photograph: Fishermen at Rio Nuevo, St Mary, Jamaica, by Mervyn Down
Cover and book design by Robert Harris
Set in Minion Pro 11/15 x 24

Printed in the United States of America

CONTENTS

ILLUSTRATIONS

FIGURES

TABLES

ABBREVIATIONS

CCESD	climate change education for sustainable development
CXC	Caribbean Examinations Council
ESD	education for sustainable development
INTEI	International Network of Teacher Education Institutions
MESCA	Mainstreaming Environment and Sustainability in Caribbean Universities
SDG	sustainable development goal
SIDS	small island developing states
STEEP	Sustainable Teachers' Environmental Education Programme
UNDP	United Nations Development Programme
UNESCO	United Nations Educational, Scientific and Cultural Organization
UNESCO MGIEP	United Nations Educational, Scientific and Cultural Organization Mahatma Gandhi Institute of Education for Peace and Sustainable Development
UNICEF	United Nations Children's Fund
UWI	The University of the West Indies

ACKNOWLEDGEMENTS

THE WRITING OF THIS TEXT represents our belief in our own moral purpose and commitment to promoting a transformative education that can move our country, region and world towards an ethic of care for the planet, each other and ourselves. This could not have been accomplished without the support and encouragement of various individuals.

We give thanks in particular for the members of the Education for Sustainable Development Working Group in the School of Education at the University of the West Indies whose work in education for sustainable development has helped to inform this text; Charles Hopkins and Rosalyn McKeown, whose significant contribution to education for sustainable development in teacher education in Jamaica helped to lay the foundation for this text; our research assistant, Tenesha Gordon, who assisted with the various phases of this research; the research participants who shared freely about their educational beliefs and practices, and their personal climate change narratives; and Thelma Baker, whose insightful comments and careful reading of the manuscript added much to the quality of the text.

In addition, we would like to thank our publishers, the University of the West Indies Press, in particular Shivaun Hearne, for their critical support throughout all stages of the manuscript development and production processes.

We are most grateful for the encouragement and support of our family – Mervyn and Keisha-Ann Down, Allicia Dunn, Lawren Murray, Yvonne Ferguson and Tyrone Ferguson.

We give thanks.

INTRODUCTION

THROUGH EDUCATION FOR SUSTAINABLE DEVELOPMENT (ESD), the global community formally acknowledged the need for an education that would transform our world and create a sustainable path for the entire community of life on planet earth. Education was identified as key in helping us address the development problems of air pollution, global warming, climate change, poverty, biodiversity loss, violence and conflict, among others, and to recognize the limits of the current development path. Education was also acknowledged as the path to help us recover the values of respect and care for self, others and the earth, for the community of life so necessary for our survival and our flourishing. Thus, 2005–2014 became the United Nations Decade of Education for Sustainable Development. It was a decade devoted to exploring the concept of ESD and finding ways to embed it in educational institutions' curricula and programmes.

Following this has been the Global Action Programme on ESD. This programme aims to extend the ESD work done in the Decade of Education for Sustainable Development and to contribute to the achievement of the global sustainable development goals (SDGs) set for the period 2015–2030. The importance of ESD is also now widely recognized and so one of the SDGs, goal 4.7, names ESD as essential to quality education.

Looking forward to 2030, the United Nations Educational, Scientific and Cultural Organization (UNESCO) has adopted a new global framework on ESD: "Education for Sustainable Development: Towards Achieving the SDGs" or "ESD for 2030". It will take into account the impact and key reflections from the current Covid-19 pandemic. The Berlin Declaration on Education for Sustainable Development emerging from the UNESCO World Conference on Education for Sustainable Development in May 2021 elaborates on this new global framework. It declares that ESD is foundational to the transformation needed to address the crises that threaten life on our planet (UNESCO 2021).

Reports from the local and global community indicate the devastating effect of the pandemic on schooling. School closures, limited access to the Internet or devices for online learning, high levels of student absenteeism in online classes, and students' and teachers' sense of dislocation have amplified existing inequities. This is a fundamental problem that has to be tackled if the SDGs are to be achieved. Quality education provides a space in which issues like these can be confronted and effectively addressed.

ESD is also interpreted within the context of the five UNESCO learning pillars: learning to know, learning to do, learning to be, learning to live together and learning to transform oneself and society. ESD is a comprehensive way and approach to learning.

Of particular importance are two generally understood characteristics of ESD: (1) ESD is locally relevant and culturally appropriate; and (2) ESD is based on local needs, perceptions and conditions, but recognizes fulfilling local needs often has global effects and consequences (UNITWIN/UNESCO and INTEI 2005). Education for sustainable development in the Caribbean, as in all other regions, shares commonalities with the global community, even as it has emerged with unique responses. A text on ESD from the region, even as it is situated in the local community, is also globally shaped. As such, it offers new insights and perceptions on how to educate for sustainability. In effect, it enhances the global understanding and implementation of ESD as it contributes a perspective from small island nations.

This book, *Education for Sustainable Development in the Caribbean: Pedagogy, Processes and Practices*, is shaped by the local context. The material in the text has been collected from three main sources. First, much of the material has emerged primarily from the local and global classrooms (including lecture halls and conference assemblies) and the community experiences of the authors. These engagements involved pre- and in-service teachers, fellow educators and practitioners, in schools and communities as well as in programmes like the Change from Within programme. These experiences offered rich examples, case studies, narratives and anecdotal experiences of sustainability and (un)sustainability. Second, engagement with and review of the theoretical and empirical literature on ESD was also undertaken. While the international literature as a whole was consulted, there was a particular focus on the global South, alongside the Caribbean regional and local contexts, to ensure that the voices and experiences of those within and closest to our context were prioritized.

Third, the text has also been informed by the authors' own quantitative and qualitative research undertakings. Quantitative research included a small-scale questionnaire of teacher educators within the discipline of education to ascertain understandings of sustainability and ESD. The research also aimed to investigate their sources of knowledge with respect to these concepts, their attitudes towards sustainability issues and their practices (including their experiences and challenges with ESD infusion in their courses). Alongside this, qualitative research was used. Three focus groups were undertaken with teacher educators. This was to further explore findings from the questionnaire and focused on their concepts of development, sustainable development and sustainable societies. Also discussed were essential knowledge for sustainability, their own classroom experiences with sustainability and real-world application of sustainability concepts. Chapters 5 and 7, for instance, share some of these research findings. Semi-structured interviews with a small sample of citizens from various Caribbean countries were also carried out to garner their first-hand experiences with climate change events. Their narratives have been incorporated into chapter 3. Having been immersed in ESD since its early beginnings, working at both the international and local levels, we have distilled our classroom and community experiences and drawn insights from the quantitative and qualitative data to offer a text that adds significantly to the body of work on ESD.

In chapter 1, we explore the concept of ESD, including a discussion of the concept of sustainable development. We further examine this transformative approach to education in relation to its conventional forms.

In chapter 2, the focus is on values – a core element of ESD. Here we examine how ESD takes this subject from the margins to the centre, from only "teachable moments" to integration into the subject being taught.

In chapter 3, we examine some of the key sustainability issues, for example, climate change, disaster risk management, peace and global citizenship. Readers are introduced to these as they are foundational issues for creating a sustainable world.

In chapter 4, the importance of teacher education is recognized, with ESD seen as essential in preparing teachers for the future.

These first four chapters provide the important framework for chapters 5, 6 and 7, which engage on a more practical level with pedagogy, processes and practices in ESD.

Chapter 5 centres on the exploration of pedagogy as ESD brings together old and new ways of teaching and learning. The approaches discussed in the chapters emerge primarily from the field of teachers' actual engagement with ESD. The new pedagogical approaches of ESD are seen to directly encourage the transformative path that our world needs.

Chapter 6 argues for an assessment that is in keeping with the differently oriented pedagogy of ESD. The chapter discusses different forms of assessment even as it presents assessment for learning as a key approach.

Chapter 7, based on recent research as well as case histories, examines processes and practices involved in reorienting education for sustainability. These narratives suggest ways to infuse or embed ESD in curricula and educational institutions as a whole.

1 | UNDERSTANDING THE CONCEPT OF EDUCATION FOR SUSTAINABLE DEVELOPMENT

CHANGING WORLDVIEW: SUSTAINABLE DEVELOPMENT, SUSTAINABILITY

Positioning Small Island Developing States in the Sustainability Conceptual Framework

SUSTAINABLE SOCIETIES, SOCIETIES THAT ARE *thriving*, are characterized by peaceful, just, respectful and caring relationships – with self, others and the natural world. That is the overarching goal of the seventeen aspirational SDGs that define what it means for our global society to develop sustainably.

The concept of sustainable development is embodied in the UN Agenda 2030. The seventeen SDGs express this concept in very specific ways: (1) no poverty; (2) zero hunger; (3) good health and well-being; (4) quality education; (5) gender equality; (6) clean water and sanitation; (7) affordable and clean energy; (8) decent work and economic growth; (9) industry, innovation and infrastructure; (10) reduced inequalities; (11) sustainable cities and communities; (12) responsible consumption and production; (13) climate action; (14) life below water; (15) life on land; (16) peace, justice and strong institutions; and (17) partnerships for the goals (see figure 1).

Balancing economic needs with social and environmental ones is a complex mission. The Covid-19 pandemic that started in 2020 saw countries grappling with this – a people's health and well-being and place versus people's livelihoods and economic interests. They are all intertwined.

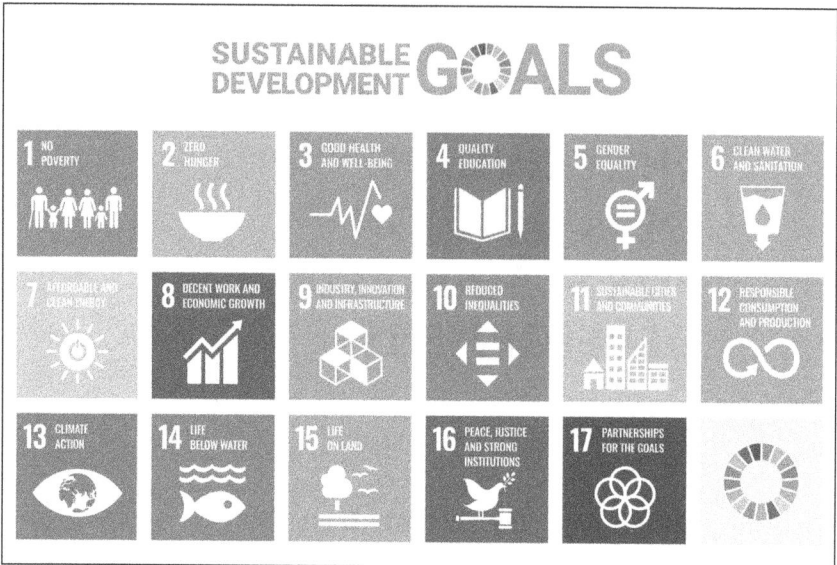

Figure 1. Sustainable development goals

Within the sustainable development conceptual framework, we measure meaningful growth by taking into account the whole, that is, the social, economic and environmental. Economic growth cannot be maintained if people and environment are destroyed or if the interconnectedness of people and place is not acknowledged. As the United Nations Development Programme's (UNDP) Human Development Report affirms, "[we] cannot protect the environment unless we also protect the needs of the humans that rely on it" (UNDP 2020, 122). Sustainable development is, therefore, a practice in which there is a balance between economic gain and care for people and the environment. Sachs (2015, 2) elaborates, "sustainable development is both a way of looking at the world, with a focus on the interlinkages of economic, social and environmental change, and a way of describing our shared aspirations for a decent life, combining economic development, social inclusion and environmental sustainability".

The interconnections of people and the natural environment are evident. People and their institutions cannot survive without a place, which is the natural environment that supports people (see UNESCO's visual representation of this in figure 2). Destruction of a place augurs loss for all people.

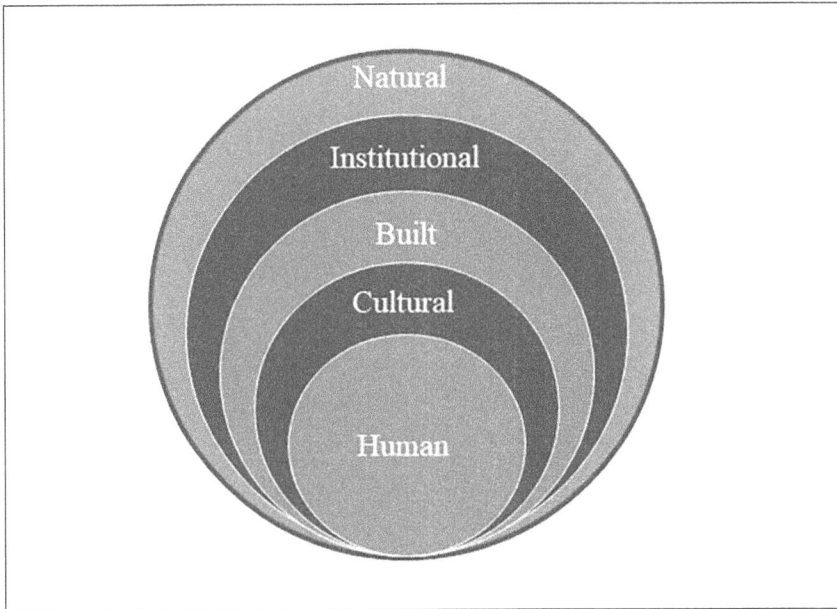

Figure 2. Interconnections between people and the natural environment

Care and respect for each other are equally important as care and respect for the earth.

These interconnections have to be understood. The social, the economic and the ecological are all part of one system, affecting and being affected by each other. Development that ignores this interfacing and fails to recognize the dimensions of a living system is a development that will implode. See figure 3 for another representation of the interlocking three dimensions.

As we consider these interconnections, we need to acknowledge a basic truth, the finiteness of the planet's resources. Our present path of development is ignoring this and heading towards the destruction of the environment and people. For progress to take place, we have to honour planetary boundaries. Rockström et al. (2009) identify nine planetary boundaries that if transgressed will lead to catastrophic events. These are human-induced climate change, ocean acidification, ozone depletion, pollution, freshwater scarcity, land use, biodiversity, aerosol loading and chemical pollution (Rockström et al. 2009). A sustainable development worldview calls for humanity to respect these limits.

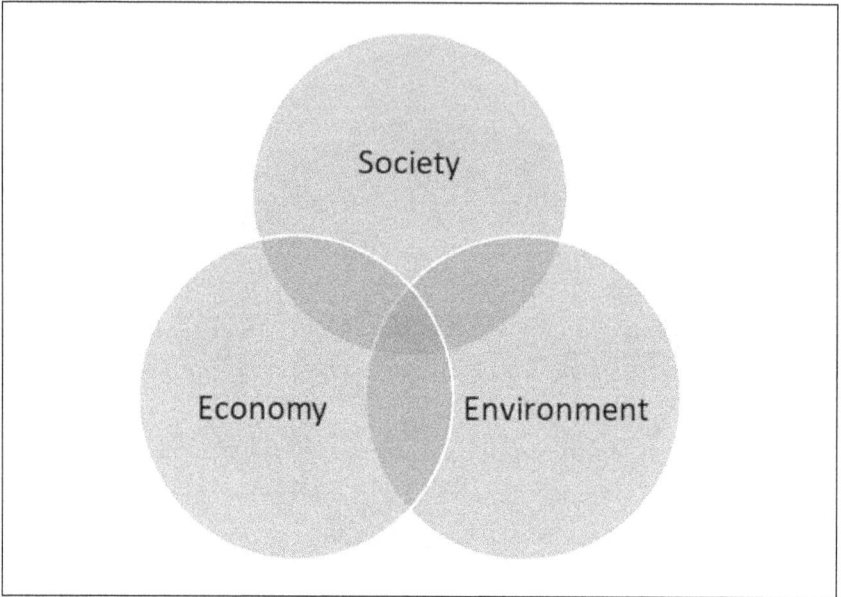

Figure 3. Interlocking three dimensions of sustainable development

This perspective has been conceptualized in various ways. The foundational way of doing so has been that of the Brundtland Commission: "sustainable development is development that meets the needs of the present without compromising the ability of future generations to meet their own needs" (WCED 1987, 43). Embodied in this definition is a generational aspect or a futures perspective. This futures perspective is also seen in the Oglala way of making community decisions (the Oglala are part of the Lakota First Nation in South Dakota, United States). They consider how future generations will be affected; they make decisions as if the seven generations are already sitting with them. And more recently, we see this acknowledgement of this wisdom in Wales where there is a newly established government post, that of a future generation commissioner. That person is responsible for ensuring that public bodies include in their decision-making process the impact of the proposed action on the well-being of future generations (Tamarack Media Corporation 2020). This changing worldview has emerged from the recognition and acknowledgement that humanity's present path is leading to the destruction of people and the natural environment.

The dominant concept and forms of development have had, to a great extent, a negative impact on the planet. That impact has been acknowledged as constituting a new age – the age of the Anthropocene – a period when human activity has been the dominant influence on the climate and the environment. In fact, humanity's impact on the environment has resulted in various development crises, for example, the climate crisis, loss of biodiversity, pollution, extreme poverty and violence, among others. This kind of development is thus unsustainable and is leading ironically to "un-development". As Atkinson (2015, 12) explains, we "live on a planet whose physical resources are finite. Yet, our increasingly consumerist lifestyles (especially those in the so-called developed world) are eating up these resources at an ever-increasing rate". Or as Sachs (2015, 2–3) expresses it, the "gigantic world economy is creating a gigantic environmental crisis, one that threatens the lives and wellbeing of billons of people and the survival of millions of other species on the planet. . . . Humanity is changing Earth's climate, the availability of fresh water, the oceans' chemistry and the habitats of other species." In the Caribbean as well as in other small island developing states (SIDS), this environmental crisis is highly visible in terms of a changing climate characterized by higher temperatures, changing rainfall and rising sea levels along with more extreme climate events such as intense hurricanes. SIDS will also have to contend with the effect of ocean acidification and shrinking glaciers (Taylor 2015). Ironically, SIDS, though least responsible for producing greenhouse gases fuelling climate change, are the most vulnerable to the climate crisis. There are also other development challenges, such as air pollution, food security issues, growing inequalities and injustices, increasing global poverty and major health issues. All these issues are demanding that we change what we believe, what we value and how we act.

The age of the Anthropocene, constituted by the largely negative impact of human beings on the environment, has its roots also in development that was exploitative and extractive of people and place. Postcolonial writers and theorists such as Frantz Fanon, George Lamming, Abdul JanMohamed, Edward Said, Edward Kamau Brathwaite, Derek Walcott, Bessie Head and Nadine Gordimer have chronicled and interrogated that kind of development. They showed in the main that the production of the Other is an exercise of power that damns both the subject exerting that power and the Other on whom it is being exerted. Freedom from such tyranny is, as Amartya Sen (1999) argues, necessary for development.

All SIDS, except Tonga, are postcolonial societies. They have had to grapple with a development that has been largely exploitative and extractive. Esther Figueroa's film *Fly Me to the Moon* (2019) uncovers such forms of development. It reveals the complexity of the development of people and place and exposes how development, specifically global economic development, can destroy both. The film traces the journey of bauxite to moon flights – bauxite extracted from Jamaica is used to make aluminium, from which the US *Apollo* shuttle was constructed. In other words, the extraction of bauxite helps to make moon flights possible. Yet such extraction has come at great cost to the Jamaican people and land.

Carolyn Cooper (2019) elaborates on this sacrifice: "Whole communities have been displaced. Farmlands have been devastated. Deadly bauxite residues have replaced the dust of the fields. Respiratory diseases have increased. What has been left behind after the bauxite and the earth-shattering machines have long gone is nothing but a wasteland. Or a toxic lake!"

To develop sustainably, SIDS will have to contend with global economic and political relationships. At both the macro and micro levels, there has to be an acknowledgement that we "cannot protect our environment unless we also protect the needs of the humans that rely on it" (UNDP 2020, 122). People belong to a place, are situated in place and so the destruction of place will also destroy a people.

To balance social or economic justice and environmental protection is a complex undertaking for SIDS as well as all other nations. This is starkly revealed in tourism, the major industry for the Caribbean as well as other SIDS. Tourism is the number one earner of the needed foreign exchange in the islands and a huge provider of employment for its people. Yet this industry also threatens environmental sustainability as exemplified in huge hotels which displace or destroy mangroves, coral reefs and beaches. Olive Senior, one of the Caribbean's finest poets, voices this quiet, chilling and not so quiet and chilling progress in the region:

> Truckers steal sand from beaches,
> from riverbeds, to build another ganja palace,
> another shopping centre, another hotel

(My shares in cement are soaring). The rivers, angry,
are sliding underground, leaving pure rockstone
and hungry belly.
. . .
Come walk with me in the latest stylee:
rockstone and dry gully. Come for the Final
Closing Down Sale. Take for a song
the Last Black Coral; the Last Green Turtle;
the last Blue Swallow-tail (preserved behind glass).
Come walk the last mile to see the Last Manatee
the Last Coney, the Last Alligator, the Last Iguana Smile.
. . . No Problem, Mon.
(Rejected text for a tourist brochure)

It is this kind of development that is unsustainable; it is this type of development that destroys the place and people who live there, despite the benefits that it proffers. Again, the question is one of establishing a balance between economic development, social development and environmental protection. Senior, moreover, exposes the recurring unequal relations between non-industrialized nations and industrialized ones, allegedly developing and developed nations. In effect, she asks what development means and for whom is this development. In the islands, the old patterns of enslavement and colonialism in which the wealth was extracted to fill the coffers of those in other places are repeated. In many cases, most of the tourist dollars are repatriated, especially from large hotel chains. The poem wails a warning "come see my land in the morning and oh but she was fair". It is a warning to the state that though there is more work for the islanders and with it benefits that such work confers, the industry, as it is presently configured, is largely exploitative of both the land and the people.

There is also the threat of loss of being, of identity. The almost comic refrain, "no problem, mon", echoing the tourist vendor's mimicry of the American tourists' accent, underlines this loss. Moreover, the refrain marks the apparent ease with which the land and the people are elided.

Global economic development, which sees the real profits of an island's produce banked elsewhere, in effect contributes to the high level of poverty in these islands. Economic globalization has also been identified by

McGregor, Dodman and Barker (2009) as a major source of external shock and stressor for Caribbean nations. There are also other social and economic challenges – high levels of social inequity, high levels of crime and violence, and these are interlinked with environmental factors especially in terms of how natural resources are being used as well as shared. A consumer lifestyle and beliefs, that see big, not "small as beautiful" (Schumacher 1990), lead to land degradation, poor waste management, high energy use and extractive industries, carried out without sufficient care of the environment. Climate change is also, as pointed out earlier, a major threat to sustainable development regionally (McGregor, Dodman and Barker 2009; Stephenson et al. 2018). Stephenson et al. (2018) further elaborate that the Caribbean region is heavily dependent on climate-sensitive industries, such as agriculture and tourism and its natural resources, and is therefore extremely vulnerable to climate change. In addition, there is a high concentration of most of the region's population and infrastructure on the coastline (Stephenson et al. 2018), which is vulnerable to sea-level rise and its attendant negative impact.

In charting the path forward to a just, equal and respectful way of development, many in the Caribbean have argued for greater attention to be paid to the historical, global and local context of the lives of the people. The question of identity has thus assumed a central position in these discourses. Respect for the self as a subject has been shown to counter or limit the image of self as other. Earl Lovelace's folk, for example, the Aldrick figure in *The Wine of Astonishment* (Lovelace 1986), come to see self as "being more, not having more" (to use the Earth Charter phrase). These figures challenge the image of self as defined by possessions, race, class or colour. Self-affirmation is, in effect, shown as foundational for meeting the challenge of unequal rights and justice.

Moreover, such selves are seen to be realized in the community. The individualism in the capitalist, materialist world is replaced by that of the individual in the community, attending to connections to the community and helping the community to thrive. The dimensions of social justice, social inclusion, equity – important dimensions of the concept of sustainable development – may be seen therefore to be fleshed out by Caribbean ideas of the self as a subject.

Furthermore, qualities such as resilience are required by communities to effectively address poverty. Swithin Wilmot (2002), writing about post-emancipation societies and free villages, discusses the development of a people through self-reliance and community empowerment. Creating communities of agriculturists and artisans as well as expanding internal trading networks and providing the foundation for new interior market towns, these new settlements flourished. Wilmot concludes that the rapid establishment of free villages represented one of the most enduring lessons from the self post-slavery experience in the Caribbean, for they exhibited the earliest examples of the dynamic possibilities of sustained self-help founded in community action.

The notion of self-help, of agency, of resilience as powerful elements for sustainable development is also underscored in David Ramphall's (1997, 21) assertion that "poor people can transform their life worlds through their agency via new social movements and mechanisms of community empowerment". This approach is also emphasized in the UNDP (2020, 21) report that states that "ultimately people are agents of their individual and collective destiny, able to drive social change". And underlying this is the issue of a people's identity. Developing agency and resilience requires self-confidence. In the postcolonial context, it means confronting the image of self as other; it also means resisting the capitalist or materialist notion of self as determined by what one possesses. It is revisioning the self in terms of being.

Yet as Brian Meeks (2005) argues, there can be no ignoring the state. We would add global markets and agencies as institutions of power that can alter the shape of communities. Equally clear is the need for a clearing where the subject positions of all can be acknowledged; equally important is the recognition of place for each subject. Meeks (2005) treats this as development and democracy joined together through open access and opportunity based on meritocracy. What is required for sustainable development is the expansion of the capabilities of people to ensure agency and, of course, the freedom to do so. Amartya Sen's (1999) theory of development as freedom is particularly applicable in this regard.

Social justice and equity are clearly fundamental to the creation of a sustainable society as the discourse on development in the Caribbean emphasizes. They are core to all dimensions of sustainability and may also be conceptualized in terms of peace, care and respect for the entire community of life. Changing economic relationships is only one aspect of moving society towards transformation. Carl Stone had asserted years ago that money and capital by themselves could not solve Jamaica's development problems (Stone 1995). Instead, what was needed was a transformation first at the level of core values. It is in holding to these values that people will come to the understanding that peace is linked to justice; that care and respect for self and others mean equal rights for all. And at that point, we can truly "imagine the possibilities for society-wide transformation geared towards equity, innovation and stewardship of the planet" (UNDP 2020, 132).

It is within this context that the role of education must be seen. We need an education whose goal is that of a sustainable global society. It must be an education that focuses students' attention on relationships, on social, economic and ecological relationships. Students will need to recognize how all these relationships are deeply connected, influencing and being influenced by each other. They will need knowledge about the human threats to the environment and what this means for the survival of humanity. An education reoriented towards sustainable development will attend closely to issues of identity, of local or global relationships; to values as part of content, and content that relates specifically to the social, economic and ecological challenges and needs of community; to connections and actions that are needed. In other words, ESD attends to these critical questions:

- Who am I?
- Where do I belong?
- How do I belong?
- What is my relationship to others and to the earth?
- How do I act?

Students are thus encouraged to consider their local and global contexts, their values, beliefs, knowledge, skills and their impact on the world. They also need to reflect on the connections that they need to make with their community and the actions that they need to take in community so that the world will be peaceful, just, caring and respectful of all life.

EXPLORING THE CONCEPT OF EDUCATION FOR SUSTAINABLE DEVELOPMENT

The Context for Education for Sustainable Development: Conventional Education and the Need for a Different Kind of Education

The overarching purpose of education has always been the development of people and places. Two education traditions identified in a recent study on ESD and quality education (Laurie et al. 2016) are the economic and the humanist traditions. The economic tradition stresses the importance of economic development as a way out of poverty. The humanist tradition embraces wider social goals such as human rights, environmental sustainability and development of the whole personality. Unfortunately, the tradition that has appeared to dominate has been the economic one. As Boyne (2012) pointed out, this conventional view of education for development had been reduced to that of the market, to education being treated mainly as an instrument of production. He lamented the loss of the view that education was primarily about the development of the person and the creation of a virtuous society.

To enhance an education that focuses on the development of a person and the creation of a sustainable society requires that we reorient conventional education. Conventional education's focus on grades and on the passing of examinations and its classroom-bound nature will have to be revised. More attention will have to be given to values and particularly to the respect of the natural world, others and self. The emphasis on "theories not values, abstraction rather than consciousness; neat answers instead of questions; and technical efficiency over conscience" (Elie Wiesel quoted in Orr 1992, 8) will only lead to individuals without a sense of responsibility to their society. Yet what is required today more than ever are "people of moral courage willing to join the fight to make the world habitable and human" (Orr 1992, 12). The call is for an education that will graduate people who are mindful of the planetary crisis, who care and respect the entire community of life – self, others and the natural world. Or, as Orr (1992, 12) has stated, the planet needs now "more peacemakers, healers, restorers, storytellers, and lovers of every kind. It needs people who live well in their places".

To illustrate further the limits of conventional education, we share a recent story of a boy's response to schooling in the Caribbean: *A boy plays truant. He is farming his father's two acres. The farm is doing well. Soon he is known as the best small farmer in the area. As a result, the boy does not want to return to school. An aunt, mindful of the importance of his education, reports his truancy to the school.*

This story illustrates some of the gaps that education needs to address. Reorienting existing education towards sustainable development can, however, enable schools to address these and so prepare students to become citizens capable of attending effectively to the complex issues being faced in this time.

The obvious reason for the boy's truancy is that he does not see the school as meeting his present or future needs and interests. The conventional way of seeing the boy's truancy is that he has failed to recognize that he needs a diploma or a degree for the world of work. Yet the diploma, the degree or "subjects passed" is no longer a guarantee of a job or meaningful employment, though the given rationale for the present focus in education on passing examinations is to make students ready for the market or the world of work.

Here on his farm, the boy is learning to provide for himself and his family, to ensure his food security and to have meaningful work. On an individual level, he is addressing a number of the SDGs. Here too he acquires a sense of self and purpose.

Of course, even the present education system, with its limitations, still has much to offer the young man. Yet a curriculum in which ESD is embedded can make an even greater difference. Let us imagine an education attuned to the needs of local and global communities, of individuals (their background, gender, abilities, interests and so on) and their environment. Such education would focus on the development of the individual and their engagement with their society. Its curriculum, set within the framework of ESD, would use the boy's farming experience and interest as the context and relate it to the content for his learning. That kind of learning would also connect him to his local as well as his global community. The kind of transdisciplinary learning that would take place would see the boy learning from mathematics, science, geography and English, among other subjects. He would also determine how to take care of his land, how to measure yield and profits, how to cope with climate change impacts on his farming, how to advocate for the kinds of changes he needs to see and how to build community with other farmers. This approach would also encourage him to bring the questions and problems he has to the classroom, and receive answers that would naturally include specific subject content.

Such education would attend to students learning to be, to know, to do, to live together and to transform themselves and their societies. These are UNESCO's five pillars of learning. Students would therefore be learning who they are. This would entail exploring their identities within the context of their various communities. They would be gaining knowledge about sustainability issues. This would encompass knowing where and how to acquire knowledge as well as how to critically assess it. And at the same time, they would learn "to do". They would be engaged in learning to take action to create a just, peaceful and environmentally sustainable world.

In effect, education with a sustainable development perspective would incorporate the boy learning who he is, what his values are, what he needs to know, what he needs to do about farming and being a good farmer and a good citizen. It would introduce him to some of the issues around sustainable farming and would allow him to do his farming. His farming interest and occupation then become a centre of interest for learning varied subjects and for connecting with the community in ways that will promote its well-being. Education for sustainable development promotes transformative learning, that is as Crowell (2017) explains, learning which has a sense of purpose, taps into the imagination and is part of a real or imagined experience.

Specifically, that young man would have engaged in learning that would produce a sense of self-confidence, belonging, agency, resilience and capability. He would recognize his significance in contributing to the well-being of his community. And his life goal would be directed towards being more and not that of having more.

When schools in postcolonial societies emphasize the development of agency, resilience and capability, they are, in effect, addressing many of the inequalities that exist as a result of that historical context. More so, they are engendering in their students that sense of belonging to place, that necessary link to caring for place and others.

EXPLORING FURTHER THE CONCEPT OF EDUCATION FOR SUSTAINABLE DEVELOPMENT

Education for sustainable development may be simply expressed as teaching and learning with a clear vision and goal of creating a sustainable world: "ESD, in its broadest sense, is education for social transformation with the goal of creating more sustainable societies" (UNESCO 2012, 12). Its pedagogy, processes and practices are infused by a vision of a world that is peaceful, just, and respectful of and caring for the environment, for self and others. So, at the core, to educate for sustainable development is to teach and learn how to respect and care for self, others and the environment. To educate for sustainable development is to engage students in learning values and attitudes and employing knowledge and skills for creating a sustainable society. The UNESCO (2005, 5) definition elaborates on this saying that ESD is "fundamentally about values, with respect at the centre, respect for others, including those of the present and future generations, for difference and diversity, for the environment, for the resources of the planet we inhabit. [It is an education which] enables us to understand ourselves and others and our links with the wider natural and social environment and this understanding serves as a durable basis for building respect." This kind of respect leads to just social and economic relationships as well as relationships that honour the earth. Such transformative learning emphasizes the overarching purpose of education as that of realizing more fully the human potential, as enabling one to be more fully human, and deeply conscious of place.

Education for sustainable development prepares learners to face, examine and address the complex issues of the planetary crisis that we are facing now. The learning content of ESD includes critical development issues such as climate change, biodiversity, disaster risk reduction and sustainable consumption and production in the curriculum (UNESCO 2020). In learning this content, students are taught to explore the interconnectedness of these issues – their social, economic and environmental aspects. The importance of context and holistic vision is acknowledged, and learners come to appreciate the deep connection between people and place. Learners develop the worldview, knowledge, skills, attitudes and values that will help ensure that our world develops in sustainable ways (Nolet 2016; UNESCO 2012).

Emphasis is placed on the *why* of acquiring knowledge. Students learn that they are acquiring knowledge for their well-being and that of their community, including their environment. Recent research on ESD's contribution to quality education reveals that ESD can provide knowledge that leads students to take action on the sustainability challenges of our time (Laurie et al. 2016). As the UNESCO (2020) brief states, ESD is about motivating learners to adopt sustainable lifestyles and to enable them to become citizens who take active roles to resolve global challenges and contribute to creating a more just, peaceful, inclusive, secure and sustainable world.

ESD involves having students in all disciplines connect with the community, learn what is taking place there and take action to address the challenges and create a flourishing community. As one respondent in the research conducted by Laurie et al. (2016, 237) states, society "does not need people that know how to save water. It needs people that actually do save water". Education is more than learning about; it is learning for. ESD is thus learner-centred as well as community-centred, action-oriented and transformative. It is teaching and learning that leaves learners inspired to act for sustainability (UNESCO 2020).

Additionally, learners acquire knowledge *in context*, so they not only learn about local issues, but they also relate that learning to what is happening globally; the local and global link is heightened. The real world is very much part of the curriculum in which the learner engages. And in that learning context, with space and time to process and consolidate how learning relates to their lives and to the future they envision, students engage in meaningful learning (Crowell 2017).

These transformative learning experiences needed for sustainability require core competencies such as critical thinking skills. Sterling (2010, 33) expresses this as a shift in thinking, as "unlocking thinking". He suggests the use of the following questions as a way of learning to think

1. Holistically – How does this relate to that? What is the larger context here?
2. Critically – Why are things this way, in whose interest?
3. Appreciatively – What is good and what already works well here?
4. Inclusively – Who/what is being heard, listened to and engaged?
5. Systemically – What are or might be the consequences of this?

6.   Creatively – What innovation might be required?
7.   Ethically – How should this relate to that? What is wise action? How can we work towards the inclusive well-being of the whole system – social, economic and ecological?
8.   Practically – How do we take this forward with sustainability in mind as our guiding principle?

Our complex world with its many challenges needs people who can examine issues from many sides, live with paradoxes and work towards solutions. In other words, learning needs to include a focus on developing "thinking", on helping students (and teachers) ask questions and find meaning and purpose. Learning is not about amassing information. Information by itself has no meaning. Moreover, Sterling (2010, 33) points out that the learning resulting from this approach will be "reflexive, experiential, inquiring, experimental, participative, iterative, real-world and action-oriented".

It is important to consider core competencies for ESD. These have been stated in terms of "acquiring knowledge that is helpful for the solution of issue-related tasks; solving issues, problems and conflicts; thinking critically; communicating and negotiating; dealing with systems; facing the future; reflecting on values; participating and collaborating; changing perspectives; thinking and acting inclusively; showing solidarity and responsibility" (Christodoulou et al. 2017, 21).

We need a curriculum that includes the exploration of values and the examination of complex sustainability issues, for example, climate change, disaster risk-reduction, peace, social justice and citizenship, responsible consumption, conservation of the environment and planetary boundaries. We also need a curriculum that includes deep reflection on the seventeen aspirational SDGs, as well as pedagogy based on the core competencies.

In many curricula, content and pedagogy specifically focused on "sustainability" have been relegated to what has been termed "teachable moments" or to extra-curricular activities. Thus, this infusion approach is limited. Recent research by Roofe and Ferguson (2018) of the revised technical and vocational education and training curricula at the lower secondary level in Jamaica reveals that ESD issues, perspectives and skills were included. However, there needed to have been a more expansive treatment of ESD.

Roofe and Ferguson (2018) explain that there was a lack of consistency in infusing ESD in objectives, learning experience and assessment. In addition, key sustainable development issues were missing. This highlights the need for curriculum developers to have a fuller understanding of ESD.

The criteria used by Roofe and Ferguson (2018) indicate what an ESD-infused curriculum would look like. They identified ESD content in terms of values, issues and skills and examined this content concerning topics, objectives, learning experiences, teaching strategies, and assessment in technical and vocational education and training subject areas. They examined issues such as respect for human life in its diversity, care for interdependent life and the promotion of the conservation of resources, which they found in the objectives as well as the learning experiences of only certain courses. Roofe and Ferguson's criteria need to be applied to more curricula to evaluate the level of integration of ESD. Moreover, expanding their criteria to include learning that is community-connected and action-oriented would show even more clearly the sustainability gaps in a curriculum that needs to be addressed.

Teaching and learning that is community-centred, as well as learner-centred, are foundational for ESD. So centred, we have an education that is aligned to reality, to what is taking place in local and global societies. There is a through-flow between the community and its educational institutions as learners connect with the community in concrete ways and in real-time. Learners are no longer isolated in classrooms studying about community. Instead, students learn with, in and for the community (Down 2010). They actively participate in their own transformation as well as that of their community.

Learning outcomes and assessment are revised as that new focus on learning in, with and for a community reveals that it is the transformed society that is valuable. So, academic success is seen in terms of the transformation of one's community, that is, a transformation characterized by "respect for others, including those of the present and future generations, for difference and diversity, for the environment, for the resources of the planet we inhabit" (UNESCO 2005, 5).

Success is seen as more than subject mastery and passing grades. Success is re-defined as creating a society that is peaceful, just and caring. With that kind of education, students and teachers experience success in "real" terms, the transformation of their societies.

Teaching and learning with a vision of a sustainable world, a peaceful and just world, and being engaged in realizing that vision and purpose will produce classrooms that are "alive" and actively contributing to a sustainable world. In these classrooms, values will be at the centre, the content will be grounded in local and global realities and will provide students with knowledge on how to be, how to live with others, how to think critically and creatively, how to learn and how to connect with community. Moreover, taking action to address sustainability challenges will be the norm in these classrooms.

Of particular importance in SIDS like the Caribbean is students' understanding of the context of their lives. The question of identity, of self and self in a community, is paramount to those who live in SIDS. Bearing the image of Other, imposed from previous "mother countries" and internalized by some to varying degrees, people of diverse groups of race, colour and class in postcolonial societies have to obliterate that image in order to discover the significance of themselves as subjects. It is from that position of seeing themselves as subjects that they can arrive at a sense of possessing agency, and it is in having that knowledge of themselves as capable beings, as having significance, that they can then begin to see themselves as being *valuable* to their society, that is, valuable beyond being simply tools of labour and production.

The desire for a society that is peaceful, just, respectful of all lives will not emerge purely from people possessing knowledge of the threat to the planet by human beings. The "Aldrick" experience (see Earl Lovelace's *The Dragon Can't Dance* [1979]) is foundational. Aldrick recognizes that resistance and transgression are limited in achieving the "good life"; the "dragon" is powerless without the knowledge that his and, by extension, a people's significance are derived from *be-ing* and not from their possessing a name and material things. Learning the significance of the *self*, therefore, has to be brought to the fore as ESD addresses questions of equality and justice.

Closely related to this issue of seeing the self as important is that of students learning to be resilient like the free villagers discussed earlier. Transformational learning needs to include that as a core element. Lotz-Sisitka et al.

(2015) question the notion of *resilience*, seeing it as simply complying and learning to keep the system stable. We expand that view of resilience. To be agents of change for a sustainable society requires a people to keep "standing up" for their rights, even after having been knocked down. Bob Marley's song "Get Up, Stand Up" powerfully expresses this view of resilience. It means not submitting, not giving in. It means that we keep breathing, (especially for those who no longer can) and struggling until we achieve. How do you teach that? That is the kind of question that an ESD poses. It points to the goals, to what needs to be achieved in the classroom and helps us figure it out. Education for sustainable development does not present itself as having all the answers, as being final – it invites its participants to centre on the goal, the principles and to continually adjust its tools to find a way through.

In ESD classrooms, learning is about discovering one's capabilities and the possibilities for agency. And it is learning to be earthed in community, its traditions, beliefs and values that are life-sustaining. So positioned, the learner comes to understand and engage in relationships (social, economic, environmental and cultural) for creating a sustainable world.

ESD offers teaching and learning centred by the vision of a world that is peaceful, just, and respectful of and caring for the environment, self and others. It is education that is shaped by the hope of human beings learning to see themselves as connected and to the earth. It is also education that is underpinned by the knowledge that all flourishing is mutual (Kimmerer 2013). It is education that leads to a sustainable society, a *good society*, one which includes economic prosperity, social inclusion, environmental sustainability and good governance (Sachs 2015). All subjects, all disciplines can incorporate the concept, content and connection to a community that ESD offers. Chapter 5 of our text focuses on how this can be done. Indeed, we need to ask this critical question: What contribution can each discipline make to transforming our world into a sustainable one? ESD pedagogy, processes and practices involve reorienting the entire curriculum as well as the practices of educational institutions as a whole.

2 | VALUES EDUCATION FOR SUSTAINABILITY

EDUCATION FOR SUSTAINABLE DEVELOPMENT AND VALUES

ESD ENCOMPASSES VARIOUS ELEMENTS AS outlined in various international strategies, one of which is values. Values – the principles, standards, ideals that are esteemed worthy – are important precursors for action and transformation. UNESCO (2006, i) proposes that "ESD is fundamentally about values, with respect at the centre: respect for others, including those of present and future generations, for difference and diversity, for the environment, for the resources of the planet we inhabit". In *Agenda 21*, the role of education in sustainability is emphasized, with reference made to values as one of the critical components for achieving environmental and ethical awareness, alongside the development of knowledge, skills and behaviour consistent with sustainability (UNCED 1992). The fundamental importance of values is underscored in the Earth Charter, an international declaration and framework of values and principles integral to moving the world towards justice, equity, peace and sustainability. The charter articulates that "fundamental changes are needed in our values, institutions and ways of living" (Earth Charter Commission 1992) to avoid destroying the planet earth, each other and ourselves. The charter further proposes that "we urgently need a shared vision of basic values to provide an ethical foundation for the emerging world community" (Earth Charter Commission 1992). As in *Agenda 21*, the Earth Charter Commission also highlights the role of education in promoting these values and calling for the integration of values (alongside knowledge and skills) into formal education and lifelong learning. Of significance, they draw attention to the "importance of moral and spiritual education for sustainable living" (Earth Charter Commission 1992). UNESCO (2006) acknowledges that education alone cannot instil the values needed to support sustainability but highlights its great potential in this area.

The pillars of learning outlined by Delors et al. (1996) in their report *Learning: The Treasure Within* are all underpinned by knowledge, skills and values. For instance, the learning to live together pillar necessitates values such as tolerance and respect in order for us to co-exist peaceably and harmoniously in our increasingly multicultural and interconnected world.

An emphasis on values is important given that much of the degradation and destruction of the earth is attributable to human beings. Indeed, "The human element is now widely recognized as the key variable in sustainable development, both in terms of reasons for unsustainable development and in terms of the hopes for sustainable development. Human relationships based on naked self-interest (greed, envy or lust for power, for example) maintain inequitable distribution of wealth, generate conflict and lead to scant regard for the future availability of natural resources" (UNESCO 2006, 15). Thus, at the centre of the current global crisis we are faced with values that are anthropocentric, human-focused and centred, and selfish (Thomas-Hope 1996). As Thomas-Hope articulates, "The environmental crisis which we face today is essentially a crisis of humankind, not a crisis of nature" (1996, 1). Delors et al. (1996, 20) propose that "the far-reaching changes in the traditional patterns of life require of us a better understanding of other people and the world at large; they demand mutual understanding, peaceful interchange and, indeed, harmony – the very things that are most lacking in our world today". As with Thomas-Hope, we see a very clear notion that a change in values is a necessary prerequisite for sustainability. Novacek (2013) rightly articulates that a substantial change in values (and accompanying lifestyles) is needed to facilitate intergenerational equity, an ethical aspect underlying sustainable development, so that future generations can live lives of quality and dignity.

THE CARIBBEAN CONTEXT AND THE NEED FOR VALUES EDUCATION

Like many other parts of the world, Caribbean nations are plagued by various environmental problems, economic issues and social ills. Some of these issues emanate at the level of government and industry. A number of these issues lie in the global culture of consumerism that characterizes the global society and that has profoundly transformed the world's value system: "The belief that more wealth and more material possessions are essential to achieving the good life has grown noticeably across many countries in the past decades" (Assadourian 2010, 10). This has translated into more greed and focus on self-interest, along with more environmental issues such as waste management issues and climate change. A number of these issues also tie into individual value systems that dictate, for instance, how we treat the planet earth – do we see ourselves as caretakers and stewards, as those dependent on its life-giving and life-sustaining processes, or do we see ourselves as those who must exploit and dominate the planet for our ever-increasing wants?

As a result, the region is faced with various issues that, unless reversed, will project us on a pathway towards unsustainability and an even worsening crisis. Violence is one of the most telling social problems that the region is faced with, as evidenced by increased rates of crime and violence, which also have now infiltrated schools in the region. Down (2015b) therefore argues that there is a need to reculture schools, and this reculturation involves a change in values, where care for self, others and the environment becomes a dominant focus. A paramount question is, Why are values not core in the curriculum? Noddings (2002) is even more explicit, asking why learning to care is not at the heart of the school curriculum. In her text on moral education, she advocates for students learning to care for themselves and insists that learning to care for one's self is concomitant to learning to care for others. She also points to the need for that kind of learning to have a clear and sustained focus.

Within the Caribbean, the focus on health and family life education traces back to the 1980s (Whitman 2004) and has a curricular component incorporating life skills and values within schools and teacher education (Ministry of Education 2009; Whitman 2004). In Jamaica, this focus on values is based on the nation's sustainable development and education agendas.

They are aimed at addressing emerging behaviours that are undermining the country's development efforts (PIOJ 2009). Vision 2030, the nation's development strategy, outlines a core set of values such as tolerance, respect, love and care, and ethics that underlie national development. The Ministry of Education (2012) has been working to infuse these into formal education. Indeed, within the country, values form part of the objectives for various syllabi in the formal curricula and, as posited by Davis-Morrison and McCallum (2003), is also taught through the informal and non-formal curriculum.

Apart from health and family life education, the civics and religious education curricula also offer opportunities for clarification and to support and engender values development within students. Additionally, arts-based curricula can foster sensory, emotive, creative and spiritual connections with nature, which is important given children's seeming preoccupation with technology and disconnection from the natural world (Bynoe 2019). Early research, for instance, on Jamaica's grades 1 to 6 curricula found that religious education and language arts curricula (as two examples) offered opportunities for students to become aware of their roles as stewards of the environment and foster aesthetic, emotional and spiritual responses to nature (Ferguson 2008a). Bynoe's (2019) research on arts-based environmental education in Guyana recommended it should be mainstreamed as the research revealed that students had a positive attitude towards the environment and the arts.

VALUES AND EDUCATION

What exactly are values and what is their role in education? Arisi (2013, 248) outlines that values are "broad preferences concerning appropriate courses of action or outcomes" and further elaborates that "values reflect a person's sense of right or wrong or what 'ought' to be". Davis-Morrison and McCallum (2003, 103) define values as "those qualities that an individual or society considers intrinsically worthwhile, and as such, proper guiding principles for behaviour". They go on further to explain that values (and attitudes) can promote "desirable character development, which influences one's relationships with others and with the environment" (103).

Lovat and Clement (2008) have stated that values education, such as moral, character, citizenship and civics education, have received renewed interest in recent times given their usefulness in addressing social problems such as sex, drugs, alcohol, resiliency education and the like. They further propose that schools are already involved in values education given that values are intrinsic to education and thus contribute to values formation within students. Indeed, Lovat and Clement (2008, 276) state that quality teaching is "steeped" in values. This is interesting given that quality teaching is connected with SDG 4 – Quality Education. According to DeNobile and Hogan (2014), values education "is a process of teaching and learning about the ideals that a society deem important. While this learning can take a number of forms, the underlying aim is for students not only to understand the values, but also to reflect them in their attitudes and behaviour, and contribute to society through good citizenship and ethical practices." Davis-Morrison and McCallum (2003) propose that values education is a critical imperative that can be delivered through the formal curriculum that promotes positive values, positive moral and character development, and prepares students to be nation-state and global citizens who are aware of both their rights and responsibilities to others.

Further, many countries are recognizing the importance of explicit values education within formal education given the various issues with which several societies are faced. Ferreira and Schulze (2014, 1), writing from a South African context, point out that schools in the country are sites "where disrespect for the law, racial intolerance and violence proliferate". As a result, they acknowledge the importance of values education in school curricula to address various issues, including, crime, violence and intolerance. As previously articulated, Jamaica is also faced with various issues that necessitate deeper engagement with values education. Davis-Morrison and McCallum (2003) underscore this need by pointing to issues of crime and violence, and the violation of citizens' rights by state agencies, commercial entities and fellow citizens. In Trinidad and Tobago's draft Core Curriculum Guide, the authors articulate that processes such as urbanization and industrialization have resulted in this belief in young persons that "everything is everything" and further that "the traditional boundaries between right and wrong, and the sacred and the profane, have been seriously eroded" (Senah 2006, 11).

DeNobile and Hogan (2014) articulate that values education takes place on three levels that intersect and interact with one another: the classroom, the school and the community. Activities can range from discussions about moral dilemmas to an analysis of the underlying messages behind particular media images. An example of this might be having students consider and discuss the following scenario: "There is one lifeboat. There are five survivors: four normal adults and a dog. The lifeboat only has room for four. Someone must go or else all will perish. Who should it be?" (Regan quoted in Bailey 2009, 129). When I have used this scenario in my teaching, students almost always unanimously voice that the dog should be thrown out of the lifeboat. But why must be this be the logical choice? Also, would their choice be different if the word "normal" was removed from the descriptor for the adults? Would there then be questions of whether one of these adults has a disability and therefore whether that adult should be the individual thrown out of the lifeboat? This scenario can allow for students to consider a range of issues such as those surrounding the human and non-human world, environmental ethics, the value of life (in all forms), the value of all human beings and considerations of what "normal" is and is not, and why. Similar to the questions outlined in chapter 1 that ESD should enable us to answer, Trinidad and Tobago's draft Core Curriculum Guide outlines that values education should help students answer four critical questions:

1. What am I becoming?
2. Is this the best I can be?
3. How can I harness all the available resources to help me to become what I want to become?
4. How will what I am becoming serve mankind? (Senah 2006, 7)

All questions are important, but the first two call for a reflection on self and the fourth pushes students to think outward about others.

At the level of the school, values can be explicitly and implicitly taught through factors such as the school's history and culture, and through schools with a faith-based foundation. Moving to the community level, pedagogical approaches such as community-learning, service-learning or volunteerism can offer students additional opportunities to engage with, develop and clarify values.

SUSTAINABILITY AND VALUES

As seen in the discourse of documents such as *Agenda 21* and global agencies such as UNESCO, values are integrally tied into ESD. Values form part of a broader framework inclusive of knowledge, attitudes, skills and behaviour. Indeed, our values are a mediating influence between knowledge and behaviour, as knowledge alone does not necessarily translate into a change in behaviour. People can know that plastic bottles are harmful to the environment yet still buy bottled water regularly instead of using a reusable container. People can know that the garbage should be properly disposed of in bins yet throw a wrapper or bottle out of a car window instead of keeping it in the car until they can dispose of it properly. Rather, values are a critical factor in the long-term attitudinal and behaviour changes needed for sustainability. Arisi (2013, 252) provides useful examples of the types of values, alongside knowledge and skills, that should be developed as part of ESD (see table 1).

What are some of these values that are integral to a just, peaceful and equitable society? Kopnina (2014) points out that within sustainability there can be various values such as values related to the environment. There are instrumental values that see the environment as a "resource" for human use as well as intrinsic values which see the environment as having value in and of itself apart from its value to humans. Note though that instrumental values will not necessarily lead to the community of care that is needed to truly revolutionize the world and how we see our place within the web of

Table 1. Knowledge, Values and Skills

Knowledge	Values	Skills
How natural processes work	A commitment to all living things	Co-operative working
How our lives connect with others	A desire for social justice, empathy and awareness	Critical thinking, negotiation
The planet earth as a finite resource	Understanding of quality of life, rights and responsibilities	Reasoned debate, problem-solving
How to make decisions, how we provide for human needs	A global perspective and loyalty to the world community	Creative ability, research and data handling, communication skills

nature and within wider society. Kopnina also points out that there are social values, such as democracy.

Vavrousek (cited in Novacek 2013) offers a framework of values that characterize an industrial society and which have led to our current global and regional values and proposes a shift towards alternative values that underlie sustainable development. For example, in his framework, the predatory attitude towards nature, which has led to our current ecological crisis, needs to see a shift towards an awareness of our unity with nature. Similarly, the hedonistic and consumerist lifestyle that currently exists needs to see a shift towards a focus on modesty and the quality of life.

UNESCO (2006, 16) outlines the values that must underpin sustainability as the following:

- Respect for the dignity and human rights of all people throughout the world and a commitment to social and economic justice for all;
- Respect for the human rights of future generations and a commitment to intergenerational responsibility;
- Respect and care for the greater community of life in all its diversity which involves the protection and restoration of the Earth's ecosystems;
- Respect for cultural diversity and a commitment to build locally and globally a culture of tolerance, non-violence and peace.

The Earth Charter Commission outlines sixteen principles and values under four broad categories:

- Respect and care for the community of life – This has as its foundation the notion that the Earth is comprised of a diversity of life forms – human and non-human, living and non-living – that are interdependent and each with their own intrinsic value apart from their value to human beings. It calls for the valuing and protection of this community of life for the common good. Humans – all of us – therefore have a responsibility to protect our planet for present generations, future generations, and simply because this community of life is valuable even if we (humans) did not exist.
- Ecological integrity – This category underscores our responsibility to protect, restore and prevent harm to the ecological processes of our planet.

Conservation and wise management are important. So too are changes in the underlying values of our world which are driven by consumerism – this drive to own, procure, get and then own, procure, get some more – towards values that are more consistent with living simply with focus on our needs as opposed to our ever-increasing wants. Importantly as well, this calls for a valuing of indigenous, local, community-based ways of knowing and living with the land, oftentimes with an underlying spiritual worldview that differs significantly from Westernized and scientific ways of knowing.

- Social and economic justice – This involves the valuing of principles of equity and equality in our current world system and within our various nations and communities. It calls us, as human beings living within a community of life comprised of fellow human beings, to fight for issues such as human rights and gender equality, and to fight against circumstances such as poverty, racism and discrimination. Contemporary movements and issues such as Black Lives Matter and the fight for climate justice represent those that should occupy our mind-sets as they call us to question whether and how we can truly live comfortably and complacently knowing that others are struggling to access water, access education, earn equal pay for comparable work, along with other challenges.

- Democracy, nonviolence and peace – With this category, we are called to value peace, that is, a way of life that embraces respectful, harmonious living with others, with our natural environment and with ourselves. It calls for an end to war, conflict and strife –which can destroy man and nature – and instead to embrace peace-keeping, peace-making and peace-building. It also calls for the valuing of participatory decision-making and governance processes that are inclusive, transparent and accountable.

These values outline an ethic of care for the earth and society that are necessary prerequisites for a sustainable world.

We wish to end this chapter by highlighting two examples of sustainability values that not only focus on the values but the values in action. The first is the example of Kenyan ecologist Wangari Maathai, founder of the Green

Belt Movement and the first African woman to win the Nobel Peace Prize. Maathai grew up surrounded by and loving nature. In response to the needs of rural Kenyan women who lacked basic needs such as fuel and water due to landscape degradation, Maathai began a movement to plant trees in 1977. The Green Belt Movement has led to the planting of over 51 million trees in Kenya. Through her ability to see the interlinkages between landscape degradation, deforestation and food insecurity, and issues of disempowerment and disenfranchisement for women (http://www.greenbeltmovement .org/who-we-are/our-history), Maathai was able to advocate simultaneously for the land as well as for the women who depended on the land. Her work underscores the values of the Earth Charter, such as nonviolence and peace, the fight for social and economic justice and ecological integrity, and respect and care for the community of life. It also illustrates the power of values in action (see https://www.bbc.co.uk/ideas/videos/the-woman-who-planted -50m-trees-with-a-little-help/p05t8p8p).

The second example is perhaps smaller in scope but no less powerful. It involves Kathy Jetñil-Kijiner from the Marshall Islands, who represented the voice of civil society at the 2014 UN Secretary General's Climate Summit. Jetñil-Kijiner did this using a poem entitled "Dear Matafele Peinem" written to her infant daughter (https://www.youtube.com/watch?v=mc_IgE7TBSY). In this moving poem, she articulates issues of climate and social justice as she speaks about the threats of climate change, which can cause her daughter and others in the generations to come to "wander rootless with only a passport to call home". She promises her daughter that

> no greedy whale of a company sharking through political seas
> no backwater bullying of businesses with broken morals
> no blindfolded bureaucracies gonna push
> this mother ocean over
> the edge

and speaks about all of those fighting to ensure that change takes place

> because we deserve to do more than just
> survive
> we deserve
> to thrive

Through the powerful imagery of this poem, Jetñil-Kijiner, representing islanders and indigenous peoples who face the loss of culture and identity if their island homes are lost, speaks and advocates for equity, justice and change. This is an emotive illustration of values in action as she, similar to Maathai, advocates for ecological integrity, the community of life, and social and economic justice.

In Summary

Globally and regionally, several issues necessitate ESD. These include a consumerist lifestyle and value system; a world in which our relationships with each other, our environment and ourselves are characterized by fragmentation, division and disorder. Additionally, there is the threat of planetary boundaries being crossed. In addition to all of this, there are also problems with our current educational institutions that undermine the potential for quality education given the disconnect that exists between students' lives and the schooling to which they are exposed. Underlying all of this then is the need for an ESD that encompasses a values orientation and that underscores the context of sustainability, incorporates sustainability content and connects all of this to students' daily lived lives within their particular communities. This is perhaps a fundamental challenge for a future of sustainability. Opportunities do exist to facilitate values education in general, and specifically with a focus on the environment through curricular opportunities in formal education. The health and family life education, civics, and religious education curricula in schools offer prime opportunities for integration. Additionally, arts-based curricula such as music, drama and the visual arts are also entry points. Capitalizing on these opportunities will be significant in bringing about the values orientation needed to support sustainability.

3 | KEY ISSUES
Climate Change, Disaster Risk Management, Peace and Global Citizenship

THE SIDS AND MAINLAND COUNTRIES of the Caribbean region have particular geographic vulnerabilities. These include characteristics such as their geographic positioning in hurricane belts and seismically active zones, scarce land resources, low-lying coastal areas vulnerable to sea-level rise and dependence upon freshwater resources (Benjamin 2010). As Benjamin (2010) highlights, particular socio-economic vulnerabilities exacerbate these geographic vulnerabilities. These include small domestic markets, limited opportunities for economic diversification, dependence on a narrow range of exports, high transportation and communication costs and concentration of populations, economies and infrastructures in vulnerable coastal areas. In addition to these inherent vulnerabilities, sustainable development – the congruence between economic prosperity, environmental sustainability, social inclusion and good governance referred to by Sachs (2015) – is challenged by various issues. Two critical ones are climate change and violence.

CLIMATE CHANGE AND DISASTER RISK

Before we delve into the basic science of climate change, it is useful to hear some stories of personal experiences on climate change-related events. We wish to foreground these voices for two reasons. First, individuals sometimes get so lost in the science of climate change that they disregard or overlook the phenomena thinking it is too complex for them to engage with. Second, some try to understand the science of climate change by disregarding or overlooking its personalized, real impacts. Individuals shared the following three stories – two from the Guyanese context and one from the Barbados context.

The Great Flood – Grace's Story (Guyana)

The Great Flood – that's how many in Guyana describe the flood of 2005. The heavy rains started on Christmas Eve, December 2004, and continued until mid-January. It was the first time we had ever experienced anything like it. There was no early warning. On the east coast of the Demerara we live in a basin and so it made it particularly difficult for us. Because of our geography we had no way of getting the water out consistently. We are below sea level. Generally, for us to drain, we have to have low tide and that meant we had to wait to drain water out. So many factors caused it to have a tremendous impact on us.

Many people had to move out of their homes. My mom and my dad had to come up by me in Berbice because where I live is a bit higher so it wasn't as flooded. They had to pack up everything, even the dogs. The entire bottom level of their house was flooded. For my parents we moved everything in their home from downstairs and brought that upstairs. It definitely had a psychological effect on my mom. Even today when it rains for long periods, she begins to worry. She often wonders, "Will the same situation reoccur?"

An Unexpected Event – Marlene's Story (Guyana)

In June 2015 the country experienced severe flooding. Within twenty-four hours 100 millimetres of rainfall had occurred. The city's infrastructure could not deal with that amount of water at once. This was compounded by the fact that plastic bottles and other garbage ended up blocking the drainage. I live on the East Bank and my home and community were not flooded. However, as I made my way towards the government office where I worked, I realized that the city was flooded. As I drove in my SUV, my wheels were covered in water and my thought was, "Can I make it through?" I was afraid to drive through the streets as I was unable to see the edge of the road and there were no road markers. The risk that I could easily slide off the side of the road was very real to me. I cautiously got through and made it to my office.

We had to make a make-shift wooden bridge just to get into the building. At my office, I have a lab where we store chemicals. The water had risen high enough to wet some of the chemicals that we had on the lower shelf, so that was a safety issue that I was concerned about. Another concern I had was the damage done to resource packages that my team and I had worked very hard to put together for schools. These included books that we were about to ship to different schools. We had stored those on the floor. The flood waters had soaked new textbooks that students could use. It had taken much time to get the funding to put these packages together and all of it was damaged.

While it was only one day of rainfall, the water remained with us for about three or four days after that because we were trapped by much larger buildings and we could not pump our water out. The pump that we would have normally used was submerged and this made pumping impossible. It took a lot of work trying to clean the space. However, all the cleaning could not replace what was lost. I felt that I lost materials which I had worked so hard to get funding to procure. I had promised to deliver these and I felt like I had somehow failed these people who were counting on me. I knew how lengthy the process to gain funding again would be. The high-intensity rainfall also meant that the workspace could not be used for quite a few months.

Where Did the Beach Go? – Ann's Story (Barbados)

I love the beach and I would frequent that area every other day. This all changed when the seaweed started piling up on the beaches (around 2018 onwards). When you look at the beach, it was almost like you were seeing mountains of seaweed. One could not even see the sand anymore. Just a whole pile of seaweed. Even when it was cleaned up, it just kept coming back. This amount of seaweed was quite unnatural. Never had we seen so much seaweed turning up on our beaches.

It was very bad because we couldn't go to the beach, walk along the sand or bathe in the water. It made me quite sad that I couldn't see the beach anymore and this was a reminder that something serious was happening to our earth. It was a warning that something bigger was happening. I was able to understand the background. I knew how the warming of the sea waters was impacting this. The knowledge of that felt like a burden and it made me sad to see what was happening. Some in the community were confused about why they could not frequent the beaches anymore and persons were quite affected by the smell. There was also an impact on tourism as some visitors to our island were not able to visit the beaches while here.

So what is climate change? To understand climate change, we have to understand several concepts, including weather, climate and the Greenhouse Effect. With the Greenhouse Effect, solar energy from the sun passes through the atmosphere. Some of this energy is reflected in space. The earth's surface is heated by the sun and radiates the heat back to space. There are some greenhouse gases, however, such as carbon dioxide, methane and nitrous oxide that trap some of the heat. Consequently, more greenhouse gases in the atmosphere mean more warmth in the earth.

Climate is a measure of the average pattern of variation of a meteorological variable (for example, rainfall, temperature) over time and for a particular region. It is different from the weather, which is the state of the climate system (usually atmosphere) at a specific time and place (Taylor 2019). Following on this, climate change is distinct changes in measures of climate lasting for a long period. Volcanic eruptions and natural changes can cause changes in the earth's climate. Human activities have amplified the concentrations of greenhouse gases in the earth's atmosphere from the burning of fossil fuels (for transport, industry, energy, electricity generation), agricultural processes, waste management processes and deforestation (Taylor 2015), leading to an enhanced Greenhouse Effect. It must be noted, however, that the Caribbean is not a major emitter of greenhouse gases.

Climate change, driven by anthropogenic or man-made greenhouse gas emissions, is a pervasive threat to developing regions and SIDS. The Intergovernmental Panel on Climate Change – an intergovernmental entity of the United Nations – has stated that "Warming of the climate system is unequivocal, and since the 1950s, many of the observed changes are unprecedented over decades to millennia. The atmosphere and ocean have warmed, the amounts of snow and ice have diminished, and sea level has risen" (IPCC 2015, 40). Globally, climate change will affect agriculture, forestry, ecosystems, human health, industry, settlement and society, and water resources (Barker, Dodman and McGregor 2009). The Caribbean region is identified as an area most vulnerable to both the present and future impacts of climate change (Rhiney

2015) due to its climate sensitivity (Taylor 2015). Taylor (2015, 10) articulates that "by sensitivity we mean that Caribbean countries – their economies, the daily ordering of the life of their people, and their natural systems – are extremely responsive to variations in climate on whatever timescale they occur". He further explains that this sensitivity is due to several key factors including (1) [the region's] geographic location, which makes it subject to large-scale climatic drivers of both the north tropical Atlantic and tropical Pacific oceanic basins; (2) the geographic characteristics of countries in the region, particularly their size and topography, which "force" population, infrastructure and economic activities into coastal areas; and (3) reliance on economic activities such as tourism and agriculture which are climate-dependent (Taylor 2015). As a consequence, the region's climate has changed in significant ways, with evidence pointing to warmer temperatures, more variable rainfall patterns, more extreme events and sea-level rise.

As already indicated, this renders key economic sectors of the region, including tourism, agriculture and forestry, as well as other critical sectors, such as water and health, vulnerable to various impacts. Increased hazards and resulting disasters are other impacts on these island nations. Hazards – climatological, geo-seismic, technological – and their impacts are increasing within the global population (Carby and Ferguson 2018). Kapucu and Ozerdem (2013, 12) maintain, "Hazards are potentially damaging physical events, phenomena, or human activities that cause loss of life, injury, property damage, social and economic disruption, or environmental degradation." Disasters result from hazards in conjunction with human vulnerabilities (Kapucu and Ozerdem 2013). According to the United Nations Children's Fund (UNICEF), between 2001 and 2010, a yearly average of 232 million people globally were affected by disasters, with the economic costs amounting to approximately US$1 million (UNICEF 2009). Additionally, UNICEF (2009) reports that every year an average of 102 million people are affected by floods, 37 million people by cyclones, hurricanes and typhoons, and 366,000 people by landslides. Poorer nations have borne the brunt of casualties, with more than 3.3 million deaths in recent decades (UNICEF 2009). Hurricanes, storms, flooding and drought are just some of what the Caribbean has had to contend with as evidenced by events such as the Guyana floods (2005) and, more recently, Hurricane Dorian in the Bahamas (2019) and the volcanic eruptions of La Soufrière in St Vincent and the Grenadines (2021). Within this context, climate change mitigation (efforts to reduce the sources of man-made greenhouse gas emissions), climate change adaptation (efforts to cope with the risks and uncertainties posed by climate change) and disaster risk management become critical.

Violence

Crime and violence are driven by various psychosocial, economic and political factors that impede sustainable development in the region. A UNDP (2012, 1) report shared that despite progress in the Caribbean, "several countries in the region are beset by high rates of violent crime and troubling levels of non-criminalized forms of social violence". These are typically directed at vulnerable and historically discriminated members of society (UNDP 2012). Sutton, Jaitman and Khadan (2017, 329) describe violent crimes as "pervasive" in the region and as imposing a "serious economic and social burden on the countries in the region". Significantly, 40 per cent of the region's population cited issues related to crime and security as the main problems in their countries, over issues of poverty, economy and inequalities (Sutton and Ruprah 2017). Troublingly, since 2007 crime has increased in several countries in the region. From their research data, Sutton, Jaitman and Khadan (2017, 330) showed Providence in the Bahamas and Kingston in Jamaica as cities with the "highest levels of assault and threat in the region, at nearly twice the world average". The phenomenon of violence has a multiplicity of causes and multiple effects – impacts on the health care system, divergence of national economic resources away from other critical sectors, outbound migration as individuals seek safer havens abroad, impediments to foreign investment and disruption of key industries such as tourism. These are just a few of the impacts.

Of interest is the fact that two of the trends surrounding violence highlighted by UNDP (2012) include violence among pre-teenagers as a mounting concern and an escalation in school violence. These trends are troubling because of the involvement of children both as victims and as perpetrators. Within the region, school violence, in particular, has been an increasing issue, with school-based violence taking place between students, groups of students or gangs from other schools, teachers and students, and teachers and parents (Gentle-Genitty et al. 2017). Jamaica, as an example, has shown dramatic increases in youth violence (Cole and Anderson 2016). Edwards-Kerr (2017, 126) highlights that "youth involvement in crime and violence represents a troubling trend especially in relation to the safety and security of schools". Regarding schools, in particular, she shares that reports from school resource officers from 154 schools on the island chronicle various activities that mirror the crime and violence in the wider society (Edwards-Kerr 2017). In Trinidad and Tobago, although most schools do not report serious cases of violence, school violence is still a major issue for citizens (Williams 2017). Acts of violence in schools include physical acts of violence as well as psychological. Like violence in general, the costs of school-based violence are noticeable, manifesting as lower academic achievement and low quality of life (Gentle-Genitty et al. 2017).

It is significant that both of these issues – climate change and violence – have the potential to disrupt education and schooling. Lost time due to damaged or destroyed educational institutions, school closures or the inability to navigate the environment due to climate change-related events such as hurricanes and storms are some of the impacts of climate change. Similarly, lost teaching and learning time as teachers address disciplinary issues instead of teaching, or students missing school days because violence prevents them from navigating their community safely from home to school, are among the disruptions caused by violence.

CLIMATE CHANGE AND DISASTER RISK EDUCATION

Given the previously outlined challenges, ESD must encompass various key areas, particularly within a Caribbean context. One of these is climate change education. Ann shared her personal narrative earlier, simply yet powerfully, and emphasized the need for education as she shared her story: "A lack of awareness is the big problem, and there is also a lack of knowledge about what specific actions we should take so that we do not continue living the way we do. No matter if you are an adult, a teenager or child we have to do something. We cannot continue living the way we are doing." Influenced by her own personal experiences, Marlene also highlighted the importance of education, outlining how she is now involved. Marlene stated, "I became involved in climate change workshops which were aimed at developing more awareness regarding climate change and Guyana's unique space due to its geographical location. This gave me an opportunity to help others to see that climate change is beyond a tale to be told. It is a real crisis that creates unexpected events that can lead us to a great sense of loss."

Academics working in the region have also underscored the importance of education as part of climate change mitigation and adaptation responses. They also promulgate the creation of safe and resilient schools and educational spaces (Knight 2015; Taylor et al. 2012).

Climate change education for sustainable development (CCESD) is a multi- and interdisciplinary response to climate change that enhances individuals' knowledge and awareness of climate change science, causes and impacts (Ferguson 2019b). Further, as an educational approach, it works to foster individual and societal changes in behaviours and lifestyles, and adaptation and mitigation capacities (Ferguson 2019b). Thus, CCESD must encompass various facets to enable those in the region to both support climate change mitigation and climate change adaptation. These include the following:

- Knowledge of climate change science, causes, impacts, and mitigation and adaptation strategies.
- Skills to facilitate decision-making, problem-solving, reflection, visioning and coping and adaptive capacities.
- Values and attitudes that recognize and support climate change justice/injustice, human rights, peace and empathy.
- Behaviours and actions that support individual lifestyle changes to reduce carbon footprints and that advocate for wider societal and global change.

This CCESD must also pay particular attention to children, as among the most vulnerable to the impacts of climate change, and ensure that educational institutions and spaces are havens of safety and resilience. A formal curriculum must therefore make space for climate change knowledge, skills, values and behaviours. Significantly, research in the region has offered some insight into climate change education at the primary/secondary level. For instance, in Guyana, Bynoe and Simmons's (2014) research included a curricula audit, a survey of a sample of primary school teachers and a desk review of national policy documents. The researchers found that while climate change is not directly addressed in science or social studies curricula guides, entry points exist for introducing climate change issues. These include topics such as weather and climate, pollution and natural disasters (Bynoe and Simmons 2014). Additionally, teachers voiced support for the inclusion of climate change in the curriculum (Bynoe and Simmons 2014). Although not focused on climate change specifically, Knight's (2015) research on the inclusion of disaster risk reduction in ten Eastern Caribbean countries was also instructive, with less than three countries reporting any progress on the implementation of disaster risk reduction in schools and "little or no buy in from teachers" (195) at that time. There is, however, a possibility that a number of the countries surveyed indicated some effort to integrate disaster risk reduction in curricula content, for instance, in Anguilla, Antigua and Barbuda, Barbados and St Lucia.

Additionally, as indicated earlier, CCESD within schools should also foster behaviour changes and action competencies in students. Although not focused on climate change specifically, McDougall's (2021) focus on the use of participatory action research as an inquiry-based, learner-centred method at a Jamaican primary school to support ESD is an interesting example. As part of the participatory action research, students engaged in activities such as an analysis of their classroom's carbon footprint, estimated the carbon sequestration of trees on the school campus, organized a community meeting to share findings and conceived a schoolyard improvement project. McDougall found that the students involved in the participatory action research emerged with a greater sense of purpose and enhanced leadership skills, and were able to produce research that had real-world relevance. Given that a number of these activities were related to climate change, her research highlights how CCESD can foster the behavioural and action changes critical for implementation.

In addition to curricula integration, formal CCESD in the region must also utilize whole-school or whole-institution approaches, in which actions for reducing climate change are incorporated into the school's teaching and learning, governance, facilities and operations, and community partnerships (Gibb 2016). In this respect, the case of Shortwood Teachers' College in Jamaica is a useful illustration.

Shortwood Teachers' College was one of two colleges involved in the Sustainable Teachers' Environmental Education Programme (STEEP), which began in Jamaica in 2000 as a two-year pilot programme. STEEP aimed to build teachers' colleges' capacity to integrate sustainability considerations into various areas inclusive of staff development, curriculum development, teaching, research and overall campus operations (ENACT 2001). Working within six areas – environmental stewardship, capacity development, curriculum development and implementation, research and evaluation, monitoring and influencing policy, and networking and partnerships, the college undertook steps to institute environmental education for sustainable development, which included elements of CCESD. In their college operations, examples included tree planting, the installation of solar panels, composting, water and energy conservation, and cultivating vegetable gardens. Curriculum development saw topics such as climate change and disaster risk reduction infused across several courses, the use of project-based learning and coursework projects on topics such as climate change. Within their governance structure, the college also developed a Green Policy that spoke to areas such as water and energy conservation, waste management and procurement.

Additionally, non-formal education becomes critical to ensure that those who have left the formal education arena or who do not have access to it are not left out, as climate change is a phenomenon relevant to the entire populace. By non-formal education, we mean education through churches, non-governmental organizations and other such entities. As with the case of Shortwood Teachers' College, Sandwatch serves as an illustrative example. Sandwatch is initially a regional activity that traces its beginnings to 1998 and an initial environmental education workshop in Trinidad and Tobago. It is a programme that brings school pupils, teachers and local communities together. These stakeholders work collaboratively to monitor and evaluate conflicts and problems within their beach environments, and to conceptualize and implement various activities to address the issues (Cambers 2008). In one regional example, students aged ten to eleven years from Hope Town Primary School in Abaco, the Bahamas, implemented a series of Sandwatch projects involving observation and measurement of various beach characteristics and changes over time (UNESCO 2010). In one instance, after some measurements, interviews with beach users and analysis of various data, they realized that an important issue surrounded visiting tourists damaging a small reef located about twenty metres from the beach. The students therefore designed three projects that would educate tourists on "reef etiquette", enhance the beach and its resilience to future storms and hurricanes through replanting of damaged dunes with sea oats, and they prepared a short video highlighting how their activities to protect the beach and nearby reefs contributed to climate change resiliency.

Peace Education

Given the issues of crime, violence and aggression faced by many countries in the region, peace education becomes a necessary corollary for formal and non-formal ESD initiatives. Reardon (as cited in Wahyudin 2018) proposes that peace education prepares youngsters for responsibility at the global level by facilitating their understanding of global independence, and their responsibilities in contributing to a just, peaceful and viable global community. For UNICEF, peace education develops knowledge, skills, attitudes and values within children, youth and adults that allow them to prevent conflict and violence, resolve conflict peacefully, create conditions conducive to peace, at intrapersonal, interpersonal, intergroup, national or international levels (UNICEF 1999). Exton and Enloe (2014) highlight that peace education encompasses various educational orientations, such as global peace education, conflict resolution programmes, violence prevention programmes, development education and nonviolence education. Whatever form it takes, it is clear that peace education is crucial for the region. Additionally, when speaking of peace education, we are speaking of both "negative peace" (the absence of overt violence) as well as "positive peace" (the presence of social, economic and political justice), in other words, education that moves beyond a focus solely on negative peace towards education that enhances and supports positive peace (UNICEF 1999).

What might this peace education look like? First, it is important to note that there are various forms of education with different emphases that can be seen as forms of peace education, including the following as some examples cited by Harris and Morrison (2013):

- Human rights education: with its focus on civil and political rights; the injustices caused by racism, human rights violations, and political repression; and issues that have emerged with more focus in recent decades such as environmental issues and their associated human rights issues.
- Development education: with its focus on structural violence; global and economic political systems; and poverty in developing countries.
- Conflict resolution education: with its focus on peace-making skills such as anger management, impulse control, emotional intelligence, empathy, problem-solving skills, active listening and effective communication.
- Education for sustainable development: with its focus on the five learning pillars, including those such as learning to be and learning to live together, which require heightened self-awareness and means of respectfully and harmoniously living together.

Peace education could be delivered through formal (schools and other formal learning institutions) and non-formal settings (for instance, through faith-based organizations, community restorative justice programmes, workshops). Drawing from UNICEF (1999), it would encompass: respecting and upholding of children's rights; school cultures modelling peace and respect among all school stakeholders; addressing conflicts with non-violence; integrating issues such as peace, justice and human rights into the curriculum; utilizing teaching and learning methods that promote participation, cooperation, problem-solving and respect; and allowing children opportunities to act as peacemakers in their schools and communities. Harris and Morrison (2013) propose that peace education should include the following essential concepts: a typology of the various types of violence, the root causes of violence, the role of international organizations and non-governmental organizations, conflict resolution methodologies, restorative justice and nonviolence. Importantly as well, peace education would ensure that schools and the wider surrounding communities would be places of safety for children.

Williams (2017), a critical peace scholar, researched school violence in Trinidad and Tobago focusing on the roles of teachers' praxes of care in addressing school violence. The focus was important given his view that praxes of care focus not only on violence prevention; they also encompass a desire to see students learn and experience academic success. Thus, peace education transcends punishment for infractions to a focus on deterring students from violence through a wider compass of care that looks to the holistic development of the student.

At heart, peace education is about transforming people's hearts. Harris and Morrison write: "Peace education programs attempt to transform hearts and minds. Peace educators want to stop the violence and manage conflicts constructively. . . . Peace education is, innately, education for hope" (2013, 162–63). In chapter 7, we will describe in detail a Jamaican school-based peace initiative known as the Change from Within programme.

GLOBAL CITIZENSHIP EDUCATION

Historically, "the concept of citizenship had a home in the bounded nation state and referred to rights, privileges and responsibilities ascribed to people born or migrated to a territory with clear boundaries" (Peters, Britton and Blee 2008, 2). Although the concept of citizenship may vary across nations, the notion is linked with various facets of civil, political and social rights (UNESCO 2015). There is no doubt that we now live in an increasingly global and interconnected society, with the concept of citizenship transcending the notion of nation states and taking on global dimensions. While Davies (2006, 5) articulates that "we cannot be citizens of the world in the way that we are of a country", she does propose that this area is a valuable area for curriculum. We too agree that its importance renders global citizenship education significant for any efforts at ESD.

Oxfam (2015, 4) defines the global citizen as one who

- Is aware of the wider world and has a sense of their own role as a world citizen.
- Respects and values diversity.
- Has an understanding of how the world works.
- Is passionately committed to social justice.
- Participates in the community at a range of levels, from the local to the global.
- Works with others to make the world a more equitable and sustainable place.
- Takes responsibility for their actions.

Table 2. Key Learning Outcomes

Cognitive

- Learners acquire knowledge and understanding of local, national and global issues and the interconnectedness and interdependency of different countries and populations
- Learners develop critical skills for thinking and analysis

Socio-emotional

- Learners experience a sense of belonging to a common humanity, sharing values and responsibilities, based on human rights
- Learners develop attitudes of empathy, solidarity and respect for differences and diversity

Behavioural

- Learners act effectively and responsibly at local, national and global levels for a more peaceful and sustainable world
- Learners develop motivation and willingness to take necessary action

Source: UNESCO 2015.

UNESCO (2015, 14) also notes the importance of global citizenship in our current world context, highlighting that the concept "refers to a sense of belonging to a broader community and common humanity", and identifying particular cognitive, socio-emotional and behavioural outcomes. These key learning outcomes are identified in table 2.

Global citizenship education is of course important in its own right, but for issues such as climate change and violence, it has enhanced significance. Human-induced climate change is an issue that calls for values such as empathy given that the nations that contributed least to the problem (such as Caribbean SIDS) are those that are most vulnerable to the issue. Indeed, it is a social justice issue for the global community. This necessitates perspectives that transcend nation-state boundaries to see commonalities among the human race. Similarly, issues of conflict, violence and peace also transcend national boundaries. Davies herself contends "a global citizenship identity is the recognition that conflict and peace are first rarely confined to national boundaries, and secondly that even stable societies are implicated in wars elsewhere – whether by default (choosing not to intervene) or actively in terms of aggression or invasion" (2006, 10). While Caribbean nations are not "at war" in the macro-level sense of the term, consider the implications of violence in the region, with just one issue – that of migration. Many individuals have migrated because of the issues of violence, aggression and indiscipline that exist in these nations. Global citizenship education then calls for the recognition that issues such as climate change and violence affect all of us by the very virtue of all of us being part of humanity first and foremost. Second, there are the impacts that can transcend the boundaries of individual nations.

In Summary

Both the island and mainland countries in the Caribbean have particular geographic and socio-economic characteristics that render them vulnerable and that pose challenges to their sustainable development paths. Two of the issues we focused on are climate change and violence, both of which, alongside other sustainability issues, necessitate emphases on CCESD, peace education and global citizenship education within any formal and non-formal ESD efforts in the region. This necessitates pre- and in-service teacher education that enhances the capacities of teachers and non-formal educators to integrate these aspects into ESD and to design these elements. As Guo (2014) posits regarding global citizenship education, teacher preparation programmes do not sufficiently prepare prospective teachers with the theoretical understanding or professional skills to facilitate students' global citizenship. Likewise, peace education and CCESD would also necessitate teacher preparation. Teachers need to have the knowledge, skills, and behaviours that they are trying to develop and instil in students.

4 | EDUCATION FOR SUSTAINABLE DEVELOPMENT IN TEACHER EDUCATION

TEACHERS ARE CENTRAL TO ENGENDERING sustainability awareness, skills, values and behaviours within students. As Wiltshire (2008, 12) posited:

> Teachers play a key role in the appropriate socialization of young people for sustainable development. It is important that irrespective of the academic subject matter for which a primary or secondary school teacher is responsible, the teacher's major overall responsibility be seen as the moulding of socially and emotionally well-adjusted individuals. The teacher needs to assist the young students to feel good about themselves; to be emotionally secure and self-confident; to respect themselves and others; and to take full responsibility for their actions.

While attention is often paid to children and youth as the future (and present) decision-makers and action agents for sustainability, the sentiments expressed by Wiltshire underscore the critical role that teachers play. They are integral for shaping sustainably minded students and preparing them as active global and local citizens for sustainability – both in the present and in the future. Further, it is important to remember as well that teachers themselves are agents of sustainable development who need to be prepared with the same knowledge, skills, values and behaviours that are being encouraged in students.

The importance of teachers as change agents – within and outside of their classrooms – has been emphasized by various researchers and practitioners (for example, Brandt et al. 2019; Down 2011; Ferreira, Ryan and Tilbury 2007; Hordatt Gentles 2018; McKeown 2014). With this acknowledgement in mind, the reorientation of teachers and teacher educators for sustainability becomes a critical endeavour. Shallcross and Robinson put forward the urgent need for reorientation, stating that "the most rapid educational transformation to more sustainable lifestyles will occur if the pre-service and in-service teacher training programmes used to educate the world's 60 million teachers (including the higher education academics who teach teachers) are reoriented to sustainability" (2014, 138). As one of its five priority areas for focus, the Global Action Programme on ESD identified "building capacities of educators and trainers" as Priority Action Area Three. The rationale for this as a priority area is clear given that educators and trainers are agents of change in classrooms and the other spheres they inhabit. To fully capitalize on their roles, however, they need to have the requisite knowledge, skills, attitudes and values (UNESCO 2014).

The integration of ESD into pre- and in-service teacher training programmes is therefore critical. McKeown (2014) highlights several means by which this integration can occur, pointing to the integration of ESD into coursework assignments, the infusion of ESD into existing courses and the development of new courses and entire certificate, diploma and degree programmes. Additionally, the utilization of the whole-institution approaches, where ESD is integrated into teaching and learning, governance, facilities and operations, and community partnerships is also a useful mechanism.

At the same time, it is in no way easy since the current sustainability challenges, such as climate change, require "a different range of skills, knowledge and understanding in order to survive" (Inman et al. 2010, 98). What then is needed to ensure that teachers are equipped and supported for the critical role that they play in students' lives and the wider society? What are the challenges that exist? And further, what are the existing and potential opportunities that can be tapped into? In this chapter, we engage with these questions. Before turning to them, though, it is useful to have an idea of some of the headway that has already been made with respect to institutionalizing ESD in teacher education in the region.

ESD AND TEACHER EDUCATION IN THE CARIBBEAN

Within the Caribbean, teacher education has gained much in the past decades with respect to addressing ESD. Notable strides and development include the following:

- The Joint Board of Teacher Education has been an important local and regional actor with respect to ESD. The STEEP project which sought to integrate what was then referred to as *environmental education for sustainable development* into teacher education in Jamaica was implemented by the Joint Board of Teacher Education and supported by the Environmental Action Programme, a joint Government of Jamaica and Government of Canada project which aimed at the inclusion of environmental and sustainable development principles in the public sector. The STEEP began in October 2000 as a two-year pilot programme in two teachers' colleges – one urban and one rural – and sought to encourage "teachers' colleges to promote environmental education for sustainable development into all aspects of their operations. . . . The project aim[ed] to enhance the capacity of teachers' colleges to integrate ecological, economic and social considerations in their planning, staff development, curriculum development, teaching, research and overall campus operations" (ENACT 2001, 1). The STEEP had six main areas of focus, namely, environmental stewardship, capacity development, curriculum development and implementation, research and evaluation, monitoring and influencing policy, and networking and partnerships (ENACT 2003). This project was seminal for setting a foundation for not only the integration of environmental education for sustainable development in teacher education but also using a whole-school approach for the institutionalization of ESD. Additionally, under the Joint Board of Teacher Education, all students in the country's teachers' colleges are required to take the course Introduction to Environment and Sustainable Development – a critical outcome of the Mainstreaming Environment and Sustainability in Caribbean Universities (MESCA) and the International Network of Teacher Education Institutions (INTEI) work (discussed below).
- Through the INTEI and their work in the region, ESD became a greater focal point for activities. Additionally, ESD research and practice was encouraged through various regional initiatives such as a conference to launch the Decade of Education for Sustainable Development in the region, spearheaded by INTEI, UNESCO and the School of Education at the University of the West Indies (UWI). Importantly, under INTEI,

the Caribbean Network of Teacher Educators was formed, as one of UNESCO's key strategies for implementing ESD (Down and Nurse 2007). Down (2006) points to the importance of the support offered by INTEI and the Caribbean Network of Teacher Educators in supporting local and regional initiatives and writes that "working within such a community of teacher educators has allowed for the exchange of ideas, expertise, and experience. An invaluable source of support" (398). Although work under the network progressed slowly in its early years (Down and Nurse 2007) and the network was subsumed under MESCA, its formation was an important step for ESD in the region.

- After learning about the Mainstreaming Environment and Sustainability in African Universities programme, educators in Jamaica and Trinidad and Tobago spearheaded the MESCA initiative, with support from the United Nations Environment Programme. With their support and that of the UWI, the first of a series of three-day workshops was convened in Jamaica in 2009 with thirty-three participants from various universities in the region. As a result of the dialogue and exchange at this workshop, an audit instrument was created and disseminated to universities in the Caribbean to identify the extent to which sustainability concerns, issues and practices are incorporated into universities' curriculum and operational practices and offer a foundation for action plans that would address the issue of sustainability in these universities (UWI and UNEP 2011). Six universities in Barbados, Belize, Jamaica, and Trinidad and Tobago completed the audit exercise. As with the Caribbean Network, although MESCA is no longer functioning, these represented important initiatives in the development of teacher education for ESD.

- Much has been carried out for ESD within the School of Education at the UWI (Mona campus). This has included the development of a postgraduate course Literature and Education for Sustainable Development, the infusion of ESD into several undergraduate and postgraduate courses (Santone 2019), and the development and delivery of a postgraduate degree in ESD (with its first intake of students in the 2019/20 academic year). Importantly, an ESD working group was formed in approximately 2013. Initially comprised of a small but core group of teacher educators with an interest in ESD, the group now includes ten individuals from different specializations within the School of Education representing a multidisciplinary core. Over the decades, the ESD working group has engaged in different activities including capacity-building sessions for teachers' colleges, projects and research with teachers' colleges, offering technical support to regional countries such as Guyana in CCESD, in-house professional development sessions for staff of the School of Education, poster presentations at outreach events, the organization and delivery of workshops at international conferences, and research and publications.

This is not meant to be an exhaustive listing of major milestones and stages but rather an outline of some critical landmarks that are pivotal for moving ESD forward. With this in mind, we now turn to look at the imperatives, challenges and opportunities for ESD in the region.

IMPERATIVES

Much of the literature on ESD outlines the need for an educative process that is transformative and emancipatory, that is multi- and interdisciplinary, and that enables a transformative, action component. Brandt et al. (2019) state that the pedagogies that are now needed to shape teachers as change agents are transformative ones. Sterling (2001, cited in Kostoulas-Makrakis 2010) also underscores that transformative pedagogies are those that will be most useful for impacting individuals' lifestyles and behaviours.

Additionally, there is the need for real-world authentic learning that connects institutions with the community and whole-institution approaches. Down (2010) has highlighted that the pedagogy for ESD should incorporate community/service learning, with ESD teaching and learning being driven by community needs, responsive to community needs and anchored in the community with teachers and teacher educators developing not only knowledge and awareness but action competencies that connect with their roles as active citizens. Collins-Figueroa (2008, 2012) describes the usefulness of whole-institution approaches that bring together not only curricular infusion and innovation but also focuses on integrating ESD into the management and operations of institutions and of course involves community partnerships.

In her writing, she highlights the significance and value of this approach in enhancing biodiversity education in teachers' colleges in Jamaica.

Of significance, Wiltshire (2008) points to the need for teachers to have enhanced emotional coping skills to promote sustainable development. The idea behind this is that for teachers to truly nurture students for their role as active change agents, they must have a better understanding of themselves, their reactions to their students and the underlying reactions to these students, as these root issues will affect their classroom interactions.

CHALLENGES

Although the reorientation of teacher education is acknowledged globally, there remain some significant challenges to this facet of ESD. Shallcross and Robinson (2014) highlight several of these, including the need for greater awareness of ESD within institutions and the development of professional development models for ESD. Concerning the first point, our small-scale research among teacher educators offers some insight. In a short survey when asked their thoughts about ESD, four teacher educators indicated that they were unclear about what ESD was and what it entails, one individual said that it was an abstract and unclear concept, and one indicated that it is a new concept that is difficult to understand. Additionally, when asked about whether they had infused ESD into their teaching, two individuals had not, indicating that it was because they did not know how.

Issues surrounding key concepts within ESD are connected with this. Several research projects that have been undertaken focused on teachers, teacher education and sustainability with the emergence of important findings. Early research on pre-service teachers' views of nature, the environment and sustainable development in Jamaica found that these individuals had narrowly focused views of sustainable development, which neglected issues such as equity, social justice, political empowerment and participation (Ferguson 2008b). Ferguson (2008b, 126) further explains, "instead, there was more of an emphasis on economic dimensions such as growth and development, or protection of the environment because of its value to current and/or future generations". Another research undertaking found that teachers had an apparent lack of a global sustainability worldview.

While their programmes of study offered teachers knowledge on the technical aspects of teaching and influenced their understanding of teaching, the programmes were deemed unsuccessful in allowing these individuals to position their teaching within a larger context (Down 2011). Additionally, research on teacher professionalism in Jamaica has highlighted that prospective teachers may not have a broadened vision of professionalism that supports teaching for a sustainable society given the absence of issues such as quality standards and teacher accountability in their conceptualizations of professionalism (Collins-Figueroa et al. 2011). Importantly, though, ideas surrounding morals, ethics, and the preparation of students for the future were present within their conceptualizations (Collins-Figueroa et al. 2011). Thus, another challenge of teacher education is ensuring the curriculum introduces students to core issues such as systems thinking, local and global perspectives, social justice, futures thinking and wider qualitative issues surrounding education.

Further, Shallcross and Robinson (2014) point to more systemic issues such as the need for sustainability to be prioritized within the educational community and by governments, the development of overarching ESD policies and general education reform to support ESD. Ferreira, Ryan and Tilbury (2007) have highlighted some similar issues, positing that ESD is not a widespread concern but rather, is a priority for a limited number of individuals. Additionally, they contend that a piecemeal or fragmented approach has limited impact and propose that what is needed for sustainable change is the embedding of ESD into the teacher education system so that it feeds into all "policies and practices" (Ferreira, Ryan and Tilbury 2007, 226). A number of these challenges are highlighted by Down (2006) as well.

Hordatt Gentles (2018) writing from the Jamaican context highlights another critical issue, namely, that there is a disconnect between the traditional role of teacher education and the transformative role that teacher education for ESD should embody. She writes:

> In Jamaica, the problem with our past and projected efforts to reorient teacher education for sustainability is they are grounded in what may be erroneous assumptions about the capacity of teacher education to engender the ideological transformation required to support ESD. This is so because here, as across the globe, teacher education has traditionally been a conservative social institution.

It has been "key to transmitting dominant cultural capital" through ideologies that are more inclined to support the status quo than efforts at reform. (Hordatt Gentles 2018, 152)

In other words, the authoritarian and traditional pedagogical cultures of teacher education are in stark contrast to the transformative and emancipatory pedagogical cultures that ESD calls for.

Opportunities

Moving forward, what then are the possibilities for teacher education in the region? Where do we go from here? We would like to suggest three main areas for further development and work.

First, to support capacity-building in both pre- and in-service teacher education, the infusion of ESD into curricula in certificate, diploma and degree programmes in regional teachers' colleges, universities and other institutions of higher education is critical. This infusion has already begun with teacher educators infusing ESD or facets of ESD into undergraduate- and graduate-level courses and programmes in teachers' colleges and universities (see, for example, Collins-Figueroa 2012; Down 2007, 2015a; Ferguson and Bramwell-Lalor 2018; Roofe et al. 2021). Within Jamaica, as already stated, all students in the teachers' colleges are required to take the course "Introduction to Environment and Sustainable Development". Moreover, a master's level degree programme in education for sustainable development, global citizenship and peace has been developed for delivery in the School of Education at the UWI's Mona campus in Jamaica. Of course, this necessitates the capacity-building of teacher educators themselves. The ESD working group within the School of Education at the Mona campus is one such effort to engage in professional development among group members and spreading outwards to the entire School of Education. Additionally, there needs to be accompanying research to understand the extent to which this curricular infusion is taking place and having an impact, and how it is working (or not working). Thus, there is much potential in this area for the enhancement of those who will ultimately interact with our students at the various levels of the education system.

Second, there needs to be greater collaboration and partnering among (1) the teachers' colleges and the universities and (2) across the five campuses of the UWI. Concerning the former issue, universities can serve as capacity-builders for those in the teachers' colleges. Additionally, universities and teachers' colleges can partner with respect to the research that is needed to provide relevant and responsive findings that can further the institution-alization of ESD within these institutions. Recently, ESD working group members undertook a collaborative action research project aimed at infus-ing ESD within selected courses of their choosing (Roofe et al. 2021). The collaborative nature of the process and the methodological approach taken can serve as a model for not only other departments within UWI but also the teachers' colleges within Jamaica and the wider region. With respect to the latter point, to ensure the regional reach of ESD, there must also be greater collaboration among the five campuses of the UWI, again, for both capacity-building and research. A starting point for this could be a special session devoted to ESD at one of the Biennial Schools of Education Confer-ences where those working in this area could come together for dialogue, reflection and the penning of a research agenda for moving ESD forward.

A third imperative for the future of teacher education regionally is the resuscitation of the Caribbean Network of Teacher Educators or the MESCA network or both. Through the MESCA network, some important founda-tional work was carried out such as the audit of Caribbean universities to identify the extent to which sustainability concerns, issues and practices are incorporated into universities curriculum and operational practices (UWI and UNEP 2011). As an institutional member of the INTEI for another five years (2020–2025), the School of Education, Mona, could receive support for reviving one or both of these regional networks and drawing them into additional international networking, further serving to strengthen member institutions.

Concerning the pedagogy of teacher education for sustainability, there are also imperatives for using pedagogies that foster system thinking so that teachers can see the linkages between physical, social and economic systems, and which offer pre- and in-service teachers opportunities to en-gage in project-based and problem-based learning. This is to allow these individuals to engage in learning which is contextually based, relevant and responsive to community needs (Down 2011).

IN SUMMARY

Teachers are critical for ESD, as they occupy a pivotal role within classrooms, engaging in teaching and learning activities with students which can support and shape these students' roles as change agents in support of sustainability within their schools, homes, communities and the wider society. The importance of ESD within teacher education has been recognized globally and has also been the focus of regional initiatives to enhance this area. In this chapter, we have looked at the imperatives, challenges and possibilities for teacher education in the region. It is hoped that this overview will strengthen this area.

5 | EDUCATION FOR SUSTAINABLE DEVELOPMENT PEDAGOGY

THIS CHAPTER EXPLORES THE KIND of pedagogy that is needed to create a sustainable and flourishing world for all. It is framed by the earlier examination of the concept of sustainable development, particularly the Caribbean perspective. As discussed, issues of identity, place, justice, agency and resilience are central in SIDS, like the Caribbean. The teaching and learning approaches and strategies acknowledge these issues. Teaching and learning for a sustainable future are core to teachers and students having a vision of a world that is healthy, just and caring and simultaneously learning, in classrooms at all levels, how to realize that vision. It is about helping students to understand the vision and to move in the flow of sustainable relationships – relationships with themselves, others and the environment.

Specifically, we will explore ways for both teachers and students to envision a sustainable world, and relate their disciplines to that vision. Next, we will discuss infusion as a major approach for ESD by discussing general principles, and then we will relate this to core subjects – language, literature, mathematics, science, geography. In effect, we use these core subjects to illustrate how ESD can be infused into any subject. Using the methodological framework of the 3Cs – context, content and community connections – a framework emerging through discussions with Caribbean teachers, we will discuss specific teaching and learning strategies.

Moreover, the approach is based on the recognition that ESD is more than teaching skills and content, even content that speaks to high resource consumption that threatens planetary boundaries. Its purpose is transformative, and it therefore focuses on "dismantling unsustainable perspectives of growth and development and constructing new worldviews" (UNDP 2020, 49). This of course includes making the learning of values (of care and respect for the community of life) central and positions the learner in the community.

VISIONING FOR A SUSTAINABLE WORLD IN MIND

Vision-making is often an essential part of academic and business workshops. Regional workshops on ESD, for example, have always included a visioning exercise. Most, if not all, institutions in the region have a mission and vision statement guiding the operations as well as classroom practices. The regional university, the UWI, sets out very clearly its mission and vision with a strong emphasis on "the positive transformation of the Caribbean and the wider world" (UWI 2017, 6). In addition to this, the UWI specifies the characteristics of its ideal Caribbean graduate which include the graduate being globally aware and well-grounded in their regional identity, socially, culturally and environmentally responsible, and guided by strong ethical values (UWI 2017). This emphasis on vision is because of the tremendous potential it holds for participants to be inspired, motivated and enabled to act. Sinek (2009), for example, emphasizes the importance of vision for businesses, insisting that leaders have to find a vision if they do not have one. In discussing educational change, Fullan (2009) speaks of this as having "a moral purpose" – that is, educators having as their goal the improvement of society. He refers to this also as principled behaviour that is connected to something greater than us (Fullan 2002). He further specifies that it involves the commitment to raising the bar and closing the gap in student achievement. Additionally, vision-building exercises, such as futures workshops, scenario analyses, utopian/dystopian storytelling, science-fiction thinking and fore- and backcasting, have been identified as one of the key methods in ESD (Rieckmann 2018). Imagine classrooms, therefore, where vision-building is part of the norm, where students are focused on the purpose of their education in a way that makes sense to them.

Such vision-making needs, of course, to exist within the larger picture of the kind of future and the kind of world that is hoped for. Miller (2003) in his impressive treatise on the masculine and feminine roots of teaching, and its legacy, especially for SIDS, concludes that the mission of schooling and teaching should be "prophetic". He explains this role as one that envisions the future of a people as noble and ethical, as constructing an egalitarian society. It is a mission that is inclusive, one that engages "ordinary people to become constructively engaged with the extraordinary issues constantly confronting human society" (410). A vision then of schooling as creating opportunities for agency and for developing capabilities is central to this treatise. Equally important is the notion that the vision encompasses rising above the depressing conditions and seeming hopelessness contained in social and political realities of the time. Miller introduces the notion of hope, transcendency and resilience in the mission of education.

Though the idea of hope and transcendency is recognized as necessary for societies' transformation, this idea has not been often expressed in the literature on education even that of ESD. Yet this is core for the work on transforming society. Visioning exercises in classrooms attuned to the creation of sustainable societies need to incorporate this vital aspect of hope, of overcoming, of affirming values and virtues.

Teacher and Students Visioning, Setting Goals, Engaging in a Future's Perspective

Visioning in the classroom needs to involve the teacher as well as the students. Teachers need to have and embrace the vision of a sustainable world, of human, social and environmental development in ways that promote the well-being of all. They cannot pass on successfully what they do not believe in. Sinek (2009) points out that if a leader lacks a vision, they can find one by looking to leaders to whom they are drawn. People are often drawn to those who articulate and affirm their beliefs. So, the aspirations and dreams of a Nelson Mandela, a Martin Luther King Jr, a Marcus Garvey, a Mahatma Gandhi, a Mary Seacole, a Wangari Maathai can become a starting point for those teachers who are uncertain about their purpose. Schools, unfortunately, do not often attend to the importance of vision exercises, yet for teachers to be effective in educating for a transformed society, teachers need to spend time reflecting on their dreams and goals for the future.

Visions need to be nurtured. Teachers will need to find ways to do this even as they face and research the harsh realities of injustice, violence, poverty, environmental degradation and natural disasters, among others. If teachers lose their vision, the students will likely flounder. To nurture their vision, teachers will need to find spaces and places where their purpose is encouraged and embraced. These could be conferences and seminars focused on ESD or spaces such as churches, temples, gardens which allow for deep connections with the natural and spiritual worlds. Personal rituals may also have to be created to keep their people's dream, their hope, their vision alive. For some, it is the practice of meditation, of contemplative prayer. Additionally, there are the arts – poetry, drama, fiction, art (paintings, sculptures, photographs, among others) that can nurture one's vision. What is being emphasized here is the need for teachers to believe that a better world is possible and that they can contribute to its formation (Miller 2003; Mortimer*[1] 2019, teacher interviewee).

The following narrative of a teacher illustrates this further:

> In reading and analysing Octavia Butler's *Parable of the Sower*, our students became engaged in the sustainability issues that the novel explored. The literary text, connecting hearts and minds, made real for our students what our world would look like if it continued on its unsustainable path. More important, Butler shaped a vision of an alternate world, a world where people could flourish. This alternative vision engaged our students on both an intellectual and emotional level. Butler's dystopian novel led to a turning point for many of them. They began to examine closely their worldview and reflect on the actions they needed to take to transform their world.

It is equally important that teachers share their vision of a sustainable future with their students. More so, teachers need to see each child as having the potential and a role to play in creating this better world. In other words, teachers need to recognize that each student brings something to the table; each student is an important strand in the weave of life. Or as Clarke* (2019), one of our teacher interviewees expressed, "each student carries the image of God".

---

1 Names marked with an asterisk are pseudonyms.

There are many ways in which the vision can be shared based on the following discussion with teachers during a recent interview.

Taylor* (2019) speaks about how she encourages her students to think consciously about what they believe, their practices and their behaviours. She also has them exploring their mindsets, why they think the way they do. Using specific exercises, like a carbon footprint exercise, she provides opportunities for them to reflect on their actions and the beliefs that give rise to them.

Interestingly, O'Connor* (2019) identifies building trust with her students as foundational to her sharing the vision and them accepting it and re-creating it on their terms. She speaks, therefore, of her seeing and treating them as individuals and not just a crowd of students. It can begin with something as seemingly minor as keeping bits of information about them that differentiates them. It could be that Errol has asthma, or Carlene's mother lives abroad. And then she will ask them about these so that the students know that she knows and that it matters. What transpires is that the students then feel connected to the teacher, and they come to understand that she cares for them, that they matter to her. The point is that individuals need to feel that they matter, that they have significance. Otherwise, they are likely to find it difficult to care for others or the environment.

For students to buy into the vision of a better future, students need to have a clear sense of self and a valued self. Teachers creating space for students to shine and so validating them publicly will make them open to a present and a future filled with possibilities (Brown* 2019). Such spaces can be as simple as that of giving them a platform for sharing research and important news about their community concerning their dreams for it. It is about teachers learning to care for their students and their lives, which is not an automatic response and, in some cases, a difficult one. Being in front of the class does allow teachers, however, to "see", "recognize" each student – a starting place for building trust and care.

In effect, teachers who begin with the vision of a flourishing world and learn how to share this vision with their students take them to the heart of education. Here it is more than learning about a subject. It is learning that aims to help students "consider their own paths for finding meaning, and . . . the ways people have sought to find meaning through community action, mutual support, and love" (Rabbi Lerner quoted in Rohr 2019). An ESD grounded in visioning will incorporate an education that Rabbi Lerner envisages as an education for the future – one in which students "explore experiences of unity, mystical luminosity and joy that are as much dimensions of life as suffering and cruelty" (quoted in Rohr 2019).

Moreover, these teachers through visioning with their students provide a sense of community, of belonging, of the interconnectedness of all – a foundation for caring about the wider community, both local and global. What we have in effect is the development of a sense of what it means to be human, of knowing in a deep sense the relatedness of all – a concept that the Elizabethan poet John Donne expressed so well in his poem "For Whom the Bell Tolls":

> No man is an island,
> Entire of itself.
> . . . .
> Each man's death diminishes me,
> For I am involved in mankind.

As teachers then, we are compelled to begin our lesson preparations with the vision, with our purpose for teaching, the "big picture". Beginning with the topic, the content for the topic and the exam is likely to lead to mechanical lessons over time. The less able teachers are likely to just make notes that they will then read to their students. In turn, the students hanging on to such notes are likely to pass exams, but their own development and that of their society would have been severely limited. Further, even the more able teacher who will consider how to deliver such content, who will think of interesting and fun activities to engage their students, who will write objectives and have a central focus for their lesson, will be short-changing themselves and their students if the critical questions posed earlier in chapter 1 are not guiding their teaching: who am I; where do I belong (locally and globally); how do I belong (my values, beliefs, knowledge, skills and their impact on my world); how do I act (what connections do I need to make with my community; what actions do I need to take so that my community, my world will be peaceful, just, caring and respectful of all life)?

Education with this in mind, with a sustainable worldview, is charting such a course. In this new world that we are creating, educators need to take seriously the fact that students leave our classrooms with a "life message" and with values that they have experienced in the classroom that have gone beyond the lecture notes, the subject content and skills they were explicitly taught. Engaging our students in constructing this just, peaceful and caring world necessitates educators having this vision, this life goal and sharing it with their students.

Incorporating the vision of a sustainable world in educational institutions at all levels is therefore paramount.

INTRODUCING THE CONCEPT AND CONTENT OF SUSTAINABLE DEVELOPMENT

Our focus in this section is on teaching and learning for sustainable development as part of the teaching of subjects or courses in the curriculum. A few institutions may offer ESD as a distinct subject. Ideally, institutions would benefit from a reoriented educational system in which there is more transdisciplinary work, and cross-cutting issues are treated from different discipline perspectives. However, most institutions that aim to prepare students for a sustainable world and so want to include ESD do so by integrating, weaving sustainable development content into their curricula or programme. This is only the beginning. To fully integrate ESD, which we speak of as infusing or embedding or reorienting, requires more than this. It will require (1) an exploration of the context of sustainability, that is, the concept of sustainable development, local and global relations in terms of development; (2) content – the issues and challenges of sustainable development, the values that are needed to create a world that will flourish; and (3) connections – connecting with the community and the natural world and taking action for its preservation and its well-being.

In infusing ESD into the curricula, courses or programmes, we usually begin by introducing the concept of sustainable development. We do this in ways that are relevant and meaningful to students. These will include students' observing, reflecting on and examining their communities (institution and home communities) and so establish from the start the necessary connection between their academic work and the real world. More so, an activity like this one will establish the relevance of their studies beyond that of passing the examination. Course work or class activities will include, therefore, students' sharing their observations and their perspectives in a variety of forms (videos, art, stories), on social, economic and environmental challenges as well as means of transformation to be pursued through their distinct subject. Introducing the concept is done in a way that opens students' eyes to what is taking place in their community, to have them identify their feelings and thoughts concerning their community. This creation of a space for their responses is important, as it will lead to students learning to trust their ways of seeing and feeling and thinking.

To relate students' study of their community to the global context, we introduce texts and other materials on sustainable development content. This content includes the sustainable development concept, issues, challenges and values. In this section, students are learning *about* sustainable development together with learning *for* the sustainable development of society, with a greater emphasis on the latter. So, students will be introduced to the United Nations SDGs and the accompanying case studies. They are expected to analyse documents and others like the UNDP Human Development Reports and the Earth Charter. And of course, they will examine various texts on sustainable development. They will indicate the topics students will need to examine. These will include issues such as eradicating poverty, equitable human development, inclusion and well-being, gender equality, responsible consumption and production, clean and affordable energy, clean water, action for climate change, decent work, peace and justice. In this way, students are provided with the foundational knowledge to comprehend and interrogate the complexity of development.

Questions to include for such examinations are: Whose voices do we hear in these texts? Whose faces do we see? Whose perspective? What do we learn about the interconnections of development, poverty, justice, peace, nature? What important details are missing in these narratives? Sterling's (2010; see chapter 1) list of questions is also very useful here.

Other issues include identity, self-care and respect. For SIDS, these issues are paramount given the complex historical and present relationships between the global north and the global south.

The significance of these issues is highlighted as they are explored in both local and global contexts. This exploration would involve students' reflecting on and examining the major challenges facing their society, for example, the questions of peace, justice as well as environmental challenges such as climate change. This examination of contexts can, moreover, lead to students critically reflecting on how these contexts shape their relationships to self, others and the environment. This is likely to incorporate the issues (race, colour, class, for example) that affect one's identity, one's self-respect and ways in which this connects to the treatment of others and the environment. In other words, exploring the concept of sustainability especially in a Caribbean society will require attention to issues of identity, of what it means to be a person and a people in a particular place.

The meaning of education beyond that of the market is emphasized as attention is paid to students' self-care and respect, qualities which help to determine how they relate to others and their physical environment.

Equally important is a focus on values as the concept and content of sustainable development is introduced and explored. As discussed in chapter 1, sustainable development is about the growth that is built on relationships of care, care for self, others and the natural world. Dedicated time for exploring values using for example documents like the Earth Charter (as discussed in chapter 2), traditional stories or literature, in general, will move values from the margins, as presently exists in many educational institutions, to the core of education.

Classroom practices that model respect and care for self, others and the environment are, therefore, also necessary. In addition, practices that encourage the forging of connection of self with the earth, of belonging to place will help to shape a sense of self and establish a respectful and caring relationship of self, others and the earth. In many traditional rural villages, caring for the land gives people a sense of dignity and worth. This notion of the self being linked to the earth is rooted in some sections of Jamaican society by the traditional practice of burying the child's umbilical cord under a tree. The expression, "mi navel string bury there" emerged from this and speaks to strong connections with a specific place, with "home". Building an attachment to place can foster, in effect, stewardship for the planet (UNDP 2020).

In modern Caribbean society, the practice of caring for the land, of working at some level with the land, has been lost to a great extent. Towns and cities, with their concrete structures, have too often eroded this connection of people and nature. Deliberately structuring time for students to connect to the natural world is needed if care for the environment is to be understood emotionally as well as intellectually. We have found that school gardens, nature walks, caring for pets, practices of composting, water and energy conservation, recycling and upcycling, heritage site visits, and campus and community walks are a few activities that can be used to help students situate themselves in the ecology of people and nature.

What also works well to ensure the relevance of sustainability is to situate the classroom in public spaces. Some lecturers have had sessions on sustainable development in shopping malls and have found that as a result its connection to concrete realities can be more strongly made. Similarly, though less impactful, is having discussions in general assemblies or town-hall meetings. Such public gatherings provide great opportunities for on-the-ground input from the community. To learn for sustainable development is to learn to take action to usher in that worldview and address the challenges that existing forms of development have produced. One way to have students so engaged is through community action projects.

Taking Action for Sustainability: Making Connections with Community

The community action project is a component common to all ESD programmes, that of taking action to address sustainability. ESD emphasizes the importance of action-oriented learning. It is identified as a key pedagogical approach in ESD. Rieckmann (2018, 49) explains that in action-oriented learning, "learners engage in action and reflect on their experiences in relation to the intended learning process and personal development". As a result, "learners are enabled to become active and critical sustainability citizens able to participate in shaping a sustainable future" (48).

We learn by doing. Schools have always appreciated this fact and acted on it at varying levels. Field trips and projects have been part of school curricula (Anderson 1999), along with service learning and teacher education (Billig and Brown 2009; Kaye 2004; Larson-Keager, 2015). What ESD offers, however, is a more extensive, deepened and holistic approach to what we may loosely term the practical aspects. ESD asks that the "doing", the practical aspect of school life is transformative of self and community. Students are expected as part of their learning to take some form of action in their communities. Action learning is, therefore, seen as an essential part of schooling in ESD-infused classrooms, as theory is transformed into practice and classrooms become spaces for the exploration of present and future social, economic and environmental challenges.

There is a radical shift. Schools become closely connected to the community. They are positioned in the community. People go to school to learn more about themselves and their community, to study how to make their community better by action research. School walls are flexible, allowing free passage between both the community and the school. As a result, the curriculum is informed by the needs of the community, and a close dialogue is established between the community and the school. The interface is one in which both the community and the students teach and learn from each other. The theory is not separated from practice, but both are intertwined leading to the individual as well as community transformation. The student-centred approach to teaching and learning which has been recently emphasized is broadened to one that is community centred.

Making connections with the community, in effect, speaks to a different emphasis in the learning process. Here students are learning not so much *about* community but *with*, *in* and *for* the community. Community-centred field trips and projects become the focal point for teaching and learning. This allows students to interact and interface in real time with their communities. Context and content come together in a meaningful way as students learn to address real issues. In this way, too, they develop their critical thinking and problem-solving skills as they learn up close and personal how systems function, how everything connects.

There are many fine examples of community action projects. There is the Sandwatch programme with its distinct methodology – monitor the beach; analyse the results; share the findings; take action (Cambers 2008). Activities have included students observing the beach and preparing a sketch map; observing how people use the beach; and noting beach debris, water quality, erosion and accretion, beach composition, waves, longshore currents, plants and animals. As a result of these projects, students have collected a rich database in beach size, composition, debris and water quality over the years. Students have also taken action such as planting and conserving sand dunes, beach and underwater clean-ups, influencing tourist developers about the fragility of the beach and relocating endangered species. While this is a programme, the actual process can be a part of teachers' regular methodology.

There is also the work done in the Literature and Education for Sustainable Development course at the UWI. Students design action projects related to issues arising from the study of their literature texts, and they carry them out in their various communities. These have included a Literacy for Peace project in which the student teacher engaged in conflict resolution and peace-making through literacy teaching in two communities; beekeeping as a means of engaging unemployed young people in a community; and school farming (Down 2010, 2017). Here students develop an action plan guide, keep a reflective log and have an in-class dialogue about what is happening in their community.

These community action projects must become a normative part of the learning and teaching; they need to be interwoven in the classroom learning activities and not an added-on section at the end. This facilitates learning as being in, with and for the community.

To formally incorporate the community action project, the visioning exercises, the learning of sustainability content and values into the class-room, teachers can begin with writing them into programme, courses, and curricula objectives. Those with ESD infused will have objectives specific to the subject as well as objectives in terms of the vision, the concept, the content including values for sustainable development. Objectives specific to the subject need also to be shaped to relate to sustainability ones. This can be determined by examining how specific subjects can contribute to a sustainable world. Mathematics, for example, can help students learn how to quantify – how to count, measure and locate and so show clear connections between people and their environment (Wagner et al. 2017). We note, for example, that through mathematics, students can learn how to acquire and analyse data, which can then be used to provide accurate information for sustainability challenges. Imagine also students learning how to measure peace indicators and water use, track water scarcity, the availability of water and consumption rates. Mathematics becomes then oriented towards the concept of sustainability. Similarly, literature's contribution to the well-being of our world can be seen in its potential for developing self-identity, deepening emotions such as empathy, clarifying values, helping us to recognize different perspectives on life, and building creative and critical thinking skills. Note also that literature can engage students in studying the environment and people's relation to it, in its various dimensions, and equally important in developing respect for all life as teachers focus on these issues in the selected literary materials (see, for example, Down 2008; Garrard 2007).

In designing or teaching a course or subject, therefore, with ESD infused, teachers will include the concept of sustainable development, the vision of a sustainable world, the related content and values. Objectives and activities would relate specifically to these even as they interlace with those for the particular subject or discipline.

INFUSING ESD IN THE CORE DISCIPLINES

In this section, we are going to explore how to infuse ESD in the core disciplines and so deepen students' understanding and practice of sustainability. Having set the stage with students reflecting on the concept of sustainable development and envisaging a sustainable world, teachers will now shape the substantive content of their subjects as pathways to a healthy society. In other words, the infusion beginning with the context will now be extended to that of the content.

As outlined in the introduction, some quantitative data were collected from a group of teacher educators in the discipline of education. These were teacher educators from diverse areas of specialization based at a regional tertiary level institution. These individuals were sampled given their positioning in a department with a small but core group of teacher educators with expertise and interest in ESD who have been working to both infuse ESD in the course and programme development and to bring about a sustainability culture change within the department. Therefore, it was thought useful to ascertain their views and experiences of sustainability concepts and issues, along with their infusion practices, challenges and successes. Most of them pointed out that while they recognize the importance of ESD and want to infuse it in their teaching, they did not know how to do this. Since ESD is not a subject in most curricula, nor is it generally recommended at the secondary or primary level, most teachers will have to consider reorienting their curriculum to incorporate this twenty-first-century educational approach. Interestingly too, in a focus group session with teacher educators, when they were asked about twenty-first-century education and their approach, they identified elements that were very much in keeping with ESD. What was missing, however, was ESD's emphasis on vision, its interrelated social, economic and environmental issues, in other words, its holistic approach to social justice and environmental sustainability, as well as a pedagogy deeply connected with the community.

It is useful to consider this process of infusing ESD into the disciplines in terms of the 3Cs: context, content and community connections. We have spoken to the context in terms of the vision and concept of sustainability as well as local and global contexts that should provide the background to the teaching of the disciplines. Content refers to the sustainability issues and knowledge that need to be merged with the specific content of each subject. The specific content of the subject as it is reoriented to address the goals of sustainable development will incorporate the perspectives, knowledge, skills, values and actions for a transformed society. Community connections speak to relating the subject to the community, of students learning to take action in, with and for the well-being of the community. We also bear in mind that we will be crossing disciplines, as what is needed for a sustainable future does not reside in any one discipline.

We now discuss this deepening of the concept in the content of core subjects, such as language, literature, mathematics, science and geography. These are to be taken as illustrative and therefore applicable to all subjects.

Infusing ESD into Language

We begin with language. It has often been said that every teacher is a teacher of language. Language use is important in every subject and may be seen as the gateway to comprehending each subject. Language moreover provides an "open space" for the inclusion of sustainability issues, concerns, skills and values. This is so, as language requires material from other disciplines (science, mathematics, geography and technology, among others) for students to learn to communicate effectively and in various ways as well as acquire critical literacy skills. We are mindful also of the value of language as a means of clarifying our thoughts and processing our emotions.

Equally important is the use of language as a tool to "construct" our worlds – our thoughts, feelings and our relationships. Through language we can change the mood of a meeting; we can transform a relationship; we can shape responses to the environment and each other. Language is a powerful tool that can help us to transform our communities into sustainable ones. Unfortunately, too often our focus on language teaching remains at the level of teaching the mechanics of the language, the grammar and structure, among other elements. Yet effective communication is that and much more. And with ESD infused we have an even broader perspective. Language can be taught as a tool for peace, for advocacy, for social justice. Key questions we need to consider are: What is the content that we will use for teaching language? Language has an "open space" for content as we discussed earlier (Down et al. 2017). The teacher can use material specifically related to sustainability issues, for example, food security, climate change, poverty reduction, land conservation and protection, conflict resolution and animal protection. We can also think about the "how" question: how do we use language? ESD's emphasis on values, peace and respect for all can be addressed here as students are taught explicitly how to use words, what words, what phrasing, what narratives to show respect for all and to create peaceful relationships (Down et al. 2017). Paying attention to word use is also an important lesson for students to learn. Whose definition is being used, what is the connotative meaning of words, what is the context, how are words used to produce stereotypes? These are necessary questions as we reflect on language use concerning the goal of creating just, peaceful and caring societies.

Content too can be carefully selected so that there is a focus on beauty, peace, love, truth, hope and trust. Here is an exercise that can be used in Language classes for creating peace, trust and hope. It is an exercise used in many places for conflict resolution. The language teacher can use it to model and teach direct ways of speaking and listening with respect, of expressing "hard" feelings and of talking about "difficult" subjects in appropriate ways.

Exercise – Trust Circles: Restorative Practice or Trust Circles in the Classroom

Instructions on how to conduct restorative practice:

1. The teacher and the students sit in a circle.
2. The teacher explains the purpose of the activity (to address a particular issue or harmful behaviour, to build trust, to make things right) and the process.
3. The teacher and students agree on the rules for the circle – individuals listen to each other and speak only when they have been given "the floor". Participants use a "talking piece", any object that the group deems appropriate, as a way of determining who is speaking. Participants speak only when they have the talking piece. The talking piece may be placed in the centre of the circle and picked up by anyone in the group who would like to speak. Once an individual has the talking piece, others in the group are to listen. The group also decides on the level of sharing and confidentiality.
4. The teacher uses prompt questions (to raise and clarify an issue, to encourage a respectful response); keeps it real; actively listens; refrains from correcting and fixing; and uses and encourages the use of the talking piece. The teacher ends circle time and invites brief feedback from students.
5. The teacher ends with a ritual, a practice that will become part of the classroom's routine.
   (See www.healthiersf.org/RestorativePractices/Resources/documents/)

The importance of such dialogue, of listening, and waiting for one's turn to talk is meaningful language lessons that unfortunately are usually treated as an addendum rather than as the main lesson.

Another exercise that encourages deep engagement through listening and speaking and will lead participants to discover insights, truths and creative ways of living is addressed in the following:

Exercise – The Communion Conversation

1. The teacher and students sit in a circle.
2. The teacher explains the purpose and steps of the activity – it is to discuss a particular issue/topic/problem to find creative ideas, insights and truths. The class begins with silence. When strongly prompted internally, an individual will express their views. Others will listen deeply to what is being said, bracketing the urge to respond immediately as well as the urge to begin formulating what they want to say. Instead, they will listen and will respond only when strongly prompted internally. And so the conversation continues. Each person is deeply engaged in the process, listening or speaking. When the group is truly in sync, in "communion", through the process of deep listening and speaking, we will find that deep insights emerge.
3. The teacher brings the session to a close by an agreed-upon ritual.
4. This is a language lesson in which students are taught to be effective communicators – to listen and to speak from a place of deep truth, of communion with each other, of minds and hearts linked together.

The aim is to develop a language for sustainability. It is about learning to communicate for the well-being of the local and global community. Language learning becomes more responsive to what is happening in the community and engages at different levels to influence that community for the better. On one level, students learn to speak and write for their community, as in creating, for example, the community billboard, "praise reports" of what is going well in their community, their sustainable practices. On another level, it is about being conscious of what and how we communicate ideas, opinions and facts. The values of respect, integrity, truth-telling and care are central.

Language learning includes also a sharper focus on "reading", on reading and viewing critically, on being analytical of social media posts, newspaper articles and other media posts. Teachers need to consider having students critique materials by asking questions about who is represented, how they are represented, whose voice is included, whose voice is excluded, who and what perspective dominates, what content is missing and what is emphasized, among other critical questions. In this way, language learning includes practices for identifying and addressing discrimination in various forms.

Learning particular language forms and styles becomes even more important. The issue of mother tongues use (why, how, when) in effect their value (and their limitations) in creating a just and inclusive society and a society based on respect is also important. It is language learning in which students are learning not just about writing the "perfect" essay for their "perfect" grade. Language learning is thus presented as a living tool for constructing a better society. The shift in language teaching is made by having a sustainable perspective, a vision, a sustainable world-view.

We can therefore infuse ESD into language by using the "open content space" for sustainable development content; studying how language can create a peaceful, just and caring society; developing effective communication skills; developing critical thinking skills; using authentic texts with real-time engagement; and using language for advocacy.

Teaching Literature with ESD Infused

We now examine another discipline – that of literature. This is treated at some length, as literature is often included in other disciplines. Additionally, the subject of infusion into literature has also been widely researched. First of all, it is important to consider the unique contribution that each discipline can make towards creating sustainable societies.

Literature's Contribution to Sustainability

Literature's unique contribution to a sustainable world is seen in the way it provides students with opportunities to develop their emotions, their critical, analytical and creative skills as well as to hold multi-perspectives. The value of literature is also demonstrated in the way readers can arrive at deep insights into their lives as well as others. Sumara (2002, 5) asserts that "deep insight is usually surprising, occurring unexpectedly, emerging from curious places. One of these curious places is . . . [the] 'imagination.'"

In our complex world today, we need more than ever deep insights and the development of the imagination. This, along with the honing of our emotions, in particular, that of empathy, supports the needed creative response to sustainability. The mind/heart meld, which literature provides, is a powerful path to the better world we all want.

In addition to this, literature creates an important space for "learning to be". An important part of literature learning with sustainability infused is that of students learning to be. Students' self-hate has been identified as a problem by some teachers. At the very least, issues of identity have to be attended to. Otherwise, these issues can block progress for sustainability. Students need to have a sense of self, a love of self to truly care for others and the natural world. Literature can help with the healing needed by so many students as they develop self-confidence and trust. In *Caribbean Writers on Teaching Literature,* Baker shares her experience in working with this. She tells us, "I have seen the way in which [literature] helps students to grow in confidence, in expressing their own thoughts, ideas and opinions. They also learn to relate to each other in a civil way, to listen and value what others have to say. There is, in fact, a parallel between students' self-development and their involvement in literature" (Down and Baker 2020, 68).

A new literacy, that of reading eco-critically by paying attention to representations of nature, of human and nature relationships can also be learned to forge new ways of seeing and caring for the natural world. Specifically, students can be encouraged to explore ways of dealing with major social, economic and environmental problems through literature. Down's (2005, 18) article on using literature to address violence speaks to this:

> In attempting to change attitudes toward violence and behaviours of violence through literature, we taught the set literary texts by focusing on their social/ historical, economic and environmental aspects. That is, we examined (1) the roots of violence in Caribbean society – when, who, what, why; (2) the impact of violence, then and now; and (3) alternatives to violence, in other words, the path to peace. These questions are explored fully by Caribbean writers who understand that unless people openly recognize and acknowledge the latent violence in their society, it will erupt in unimaginable ways.

In further reflecting on the issue of violence about specific texts studied, Down notes that students "came to understand the systemic nature of violence – how all aspects of society interconnect and impact each other". Down (2005, 19) further adds, "To illustrate this is Lorna Goodison's highly moving poem 'The Woman Speaks to the Man Who Has Employed Her Son'." The absent father, the single mother with few resources, the substitute father figure, the community don who prepares the son for a life of crime, and an indifferent society are brought together in the poem. The poet uncovers the web of relationships, marked by loss of caring connections to self, other and place, that lead to violence.

Through literature, major issues like that of violence can be addressed. Students and society can find the paths to peace as they engage in the study of prose fiction, poetry and drama.

Literature Practices for Sustainability

This section details specific practices and activities in which ESD is infused in the content of literature teaching and learning.

1. Learn to read the landscape. Introduce students to the concept and vision of sustainability, have them observe their own environment, noting what needs to be transformed and what is being transformed. Have them document these observations in photos or videos. Include also walkabouts on their campus or community with a checklist on sustainability challenges and practices. Follow these with a discussion on the challenges and practices of sustainable development. Consider focusing on one or two major issues that have emerged in the study of the literature texts that have been selected.

2. Use the interpretive practice of the "commonplace book" approach, described so well in Sumara's text (*Why Reading Literature in School Still Matters*). This approach encourages multiple readings of the text; students are invited to respond to the text on the actual pages. They create a commonplace book. They make comments, notes, ask questions, give their impressions, write their experiences, and reference quotes and common sayings, on the pages of the novel, play or poem that they are reading. They are asked also to add newspaper clippings or any other material that they may find relevant. They explore how the particular text being studied influences their reading of other texts on the subject and also how the extra-textual material changes their response to this text.

With each reading, a different coloured ink is used to record responses. After two or more weeks of doing this, students share their extra-textual material and other responses to the text. These comments, notes and other "texts" provide a rich layer of meaning. Students are thus engaged in delving deep into the text. More so, as students trace changes in their responses, they can identify their interpretive practices. And most important, they become aware that their identity is being forged through ongoing relations to events and people, real or imagined (Down 2003).

3. Balance the student-centred approach with the community-centred approach. Students focus then on developing their community. They are invited to learn in, with and for their community. In practical terms, the themes they explore in the literature texts are explored in another way at various levels in the community, for example, having conversations with community members, having community members join classes for discussion and presentation.

4. Have students create conversations and situations which parallel those in the text being explored or create alternate narratives; map journeys of beliefs, feelings and attitudes as they read through a novel; "deconstruct" the text for themselves. This involves the students interrogating the text, using, for example, different entry points (gender, race, place); charting the structure of the novel and its impact; and reflecting on how it may have influenced their thinking, beliefs and attitudes.

5. Have a "town-hall" meeting in a public space (can also be online) to discuss issues being studied in the texts.

What, in effect, is shown here are many ways in which infusion can be done and can apply to all subjects:

1. Relate learning to real life, merge the study of the subject with the study of sustainability – the social, economic and physical landscape.

2. Encourage interpretive practices and have students map how their interpretive practices are formed and changed as they track their responses to various texts and events.

3. Develop a community-centred approach to teaching. Balance this with the constructivist student-centred approach. Students will then learn to think about the development of their local and global community.

4. Have students interrogate the texts and material used in class using different perspectives – gender, race and place, for example. Have them also consider how the selected class materials influence their thinking, beliefs and attitudes.

5. Use public spaces, such as shopping malls and parks, to discuss sustainability issues. And so extend the classroom into community.

We now look briefly at other core disciplines and how ESD has been infused in them.

ESD-Infused Mathematics, Science, Geography and Technology

The Contribution of Mathematics to Sustainability

Mathematics' contribution to sustainability may be seen in its overarching goal of making clear connections between people and their environments, through measuring, locating and counting (Wagner et al. 2017). Ernest's perspective of mathematics as possessing "the three capabilities of functional numeracy, practical and work-related knowledge and skills, and advanced specialist knowledge of mathematics" to be used in life beyond school points to the subject's real-life connection, which is an important aspect of ESD (Ernest 2005, 1). Hendrickson (1974), on the other hand, speaks to the merging of the basic functionality of mathematics, as he also locates the subject in a real-world context, with a "sustainability" worldview. He discusses learning mathematics as a means of acquiring the skills of critical thinking, problem identification and problem-solving. He argues for mathematics learning to solve the problems in industry, in health, in human interactions, for example, in housing, in food production and the physical environment. This perspective is similar to that of Wagner et al. (2017).

What is evident in these discussions on mathematics is that the sustainability concerns of the community are merged with the specific objectives of the subject. Attending to the context of sustainability, the teacher ensures that the subject's objectives and lesson plans reflect this. In effect, the teacher organizes for the subject's processes and procedures to be taught concerning social, economic and environmental matters. Additionally, real data are incorporated into the lessons. As Wagner et al. (2017, 44) insist, "If mathematics is to support engaged citizenship and develop an understanding of the complex systems related to sustainability (systems thinking), then it is important to use real and complex contexts for the teaching of mathematics at every level." They advocate using data from sources such as the World Bank, Global Peace Index, Water Footprint Network, Global Footprint Network, among others, in teaching mathematics so that application to real life is assured.

As with the other disciplines discussed so far, the teaching of mathematics can also incorporate the teaching of values. The context provided for the learning of quantifying goods can direct students to consider the values of justice, of human rights. Consider, for example, students analysing data to arrive at levels of carbon emissions in industrialized nations and the effect of those emissions. The question of values could emerge in discussions related to what underlies such high levels of consumption and the refusal to change, even when that change is needed to reduce the destruction of other nations.

Mathematics for sustainable societies can also be seen in activities that engage students in applying mathematical principles and procedures to addressing the SDGs. Imagine students learning how to measure and quantify energy and water use, for example, in a context that leads to their understanding of the need to conserve energy, water. We recall the work being done in Seaton Primary School in Devon, England, the school that won an Ashden Award for Sustainable Energy in 2007, where students learn in their mathematics sessions, for example, to quantify and track energy generated by the school's wind turbines. Consider also how the boy playing truant, in the earlier narrative in our text, could benefit from mathematics lessons that helped him to use graphs to study the agricultural yields in his community and its relation to sustainable land use or to monitor natural disasters and their effect on farming. Children in these instances learn about sustainability and acquire mathematical tools to help them live sustainably.

ESD Infused in Science

People have often depended on science to explain the causes and the facts for different phenomena, to discover ways of improving life. Ronald Johnston et al. (2017) make the point that scientific discovery and innovation have played a significant role in the general improvement of the human condition. They point to the role of science as a way of understanding our place in the environment and our interactions with it. In infusing ESD into science they propose that science should be located in a human narrative which will allow "learners to connect with the [scientific] process" (73).

A concrete example illustrates the point – a conventional science question or topic may ask: What biological factors other than pesticides might be responsible for bee population decline? However, with an ESD perspective, it becomes, "If the use of pesticides was discontinued or reduced, how do you think this would affect world agriculture and global food security?" (82). The study of biological factors is linked to the social and economic world. Of course, this could be extended even further to include the environmental element, as students could be encouraged to focus on the bees and their link to the human population.

The question of ethics is also an important dimension to include in the teaching and learning of science. Science teachers need to acknowledge the limitations of science, as it does not deal in absolutes as thought in an earlier time. Johnston et al. (2017) affirm that science participates in the uncertainties and sometimes unintended consequences of its own creation. Students need to be encouraged, therefore, to develop a critical response to the subject and to value other perspectives.

Connecting science learning to real life, to students' experiences, to local and global contexts as well as including reflection and a call to action are key elements. Another example of infusion in science makes this clear:

> Sustainable development issue: Non-biodegradability
>
> Curriculum: Long-term pollution cycles; Fractional distillation; Bioplastics
>
> ESD question: Where does plastic come from? Are all plastics the same? What are the links between plastic manufacture and fossil fuel use? What is the nature of the end-of-life plastics disposal problem?
>
> Student action and research: What can science do to promote sustainable practices?
>
> (Johnston et al. 2017, 83)

The topic of the lesson is "plastics" including the general properties of plastics and the uses of polythene. An ESD input would include having students explore the links between plastic manufacture and fossil fuel use, the nature of the end-of-life plastics disposal problem (see Johnston et al. 2017). In this way, a sustainable development issue is infused in the general teaching of the subject.

Or the topic of climate change is introduced as more than the basic scientific process. Students are encouraged to consider the "values" component – the lack of respect and care for the earth as a human activity contributes greatly to changing the climate and in turn changing and destroying the lives of others. The issue of equity could also be addressed as the teacher explores the places and the people most affected by climate change and how that impacts their social and economic lives. Scientific processes are thus situated in the human and more than human narratives.

Infusing ESD into Information Technology

The following response from a participant in a focus group interview on ESD speaks to teaching information technology. She identifies key points in the class discussion on "the use of technologies":

1. Professional and unprofessional ways and the kinds of repercussions
2. Copyright laws – the common situation of individuals who will copy a movie or a CD
3. The use of social media and the number of people who have inappropriately used Twitter and Facebook and have lost their jobs because of it
4. The intrusiveness of these modern technologies such as smartphones and what they can and cannot do
5. The role of information technology in sexting
6. Information technology and its cutting-edge tools, innovative solutions, its advantages and disadvantages

In examining the discussion points, we note that the content here clearly draws on real-life situations, on local and global knowledge even as it looks at the specificities of the subject. This is reflective of an ESD input. Yet further infusion of ESD could lead to a deeper exploration of social or economic issues, such as questions of equity – who "owns" the technology? Who uses it? There are also underpinning cultural issues, for example, how are social relationships reshaped? What cultural norms are changed? Then there are environmental issues, for example, that of waste: How is information technology equipment disposed of? Or land degradation: How does some information technology equipment impact land use or the landscape?

Infusing ESD into Geography

Geography helps us to understand people and place interconnections, place and people shaping each other. Students, therefore, learn how the social, economic and environmental interface, how these frame sustainability issues. They also learn to understand the importance of spatial patterns, locations and their impact on human social grouping and the physical environment. Moreover, through geography, students learn to pay attention to natural resources and their sustainability index. Field trips, so much a part of geography lessons, create opportunities for the appreciation and study of the interface between the natural environment and the socio-economic one.

Learning to read and create maps and other visual representations of information, students are taught to grasp information holistically, to recognize systems and networks. In this way, they learn how to determine the actions needed for safe and healthy environments.

Learning to read the landscape is another way in which students in geography classes can be introduced to observing their environment to identify what needs to be transformed and what is being transformed. With a checklist on sustainability challenges and practices, students are provided with the opportunity for walkabouts on their campus or in their community. They complete their checklist and document their observations in photos, videos, posters or briefs. They then discuss these and relate their findings to the challenges and practices of sustainable development. Focusing on one or two major issues that have emerged in their study they can then generate ideas for solutions to these issues.

An example of infusion in the content of geography lessons can be seen in the work done by Lausselet et al. (2017) on embedding ESD into geography. Here Lausselet is writing about embedding ESD into textbooks. Yet what is being said applies equally to lessons.

An Example of Infusing ESD into Geography

THE TOPIC: "NATURAL HAZARDS"

Lausselet et al. indicate how ESD can be infused into the topic of natural hazards by introducing a more critical perspective, that of the interrelation of people and their natural environments. The impact of natural hazards is thus examined concerning human activity. Human beings are seen not just as victims of these but also contributors to natural hazards. In learning about landslides (their natural dimensions – slope, rainfall, type of vegetation, for example) students are encouraged to note how human activities such as deforestation or the digging of a road can destabilize the fragile equilibrium of the slope. They learn that the interrelation between people and their natural environment is a complex one. A tourism industry that provides needed economic benefits for people can destroy ecosystems that protect a coastline and remove the natural protection they offer against hurricanes and tsunamis (Lausselet et al. 2017, 110–11).

With ESD infused into the geography lessons, students develop a sustainability perspective and critical-thinking skills, acquire knowledge of critical development issues, and can clarify values so that the vision of a sustainable world may be realized.

KEY COMPETENCIES

We include here a list of key competencies for ESD that need to be considered as we incorporate sustainable development into our classrooms. This is a list of generally agreed-upon competencies in the ESD literature, as a recent UNESCO publication has identified (Leicht, Heiss and Byun 2018):

- Systems thinking competency: the ability to recognize and understand relationships, to analyse complex systems, to perceive the ways in which systems are embedded within different domains and different scales, and to deal with uncertainty;
- Anticipatory competency: the ability to understand and evaluate multiple futures – possible, probable and desirable – and to create one's own visions for the future, to apply the precautionary principle, to assess the consequences of actions, and to deal with risks and changes;

- Normative competency: the ability to understand and reflect on the norms and values that underlie one's actions and to negotiate sustainability values, principles, goals and targets, in a context of conflicts of interests and trade-offs, uncertain knowledge and contradictions;
- Strategic competency: the ability to collectively develop and implement innovative actions that further sustainability at the local level and further afield;
- Collaboration competency: the ability to learn from others; understand and respect the needs, perspectives and actions of others (empathy); understand, relate to and be sensitive to others (empathic leadership); deal with conflicts in a group; and facilitate collaborative and participatory problem-solving;
- Critical thinking competency: the ability to question norms, practices and opinions; reflect on own one's values, perceptions and actions; and take a position in the sustainability discourse;
- Self-awareness competency: the ability to reflect on one's own role in the local community and (global) society, continually evaluate and further motivate one's actions, and deal with one's feelings and desires;
- Integrated problem-solving competency: the overarching ability to apply different problem-solving frameworks to complex sustainability problems and develop viable, inclusive and equitable solutions that promote sustainable development – integrating the above-mentioned competencies. (Rieckmann 2018, 44–45)

In Summary

To infuse ESD into our curricula and educational programmes we need to:

- Align topics with sustainable development goals, issues and vision (for example, social justice issues, poverty, crime and violence, environmental degradation, climate change). Engage students in visioning exercises – have them imagine what a sustainable society would look like. Help them to see the purpose of learning the subject being taught, in terms of its contribution to transforming society into a peaceful, just and caring one.
- Use the three dimensions of ESD – social, economic and environmental

to explore topics and note their interrelatedness. Note also the cultural underpinnings. Examine relations of humans and nature; and humans and humans.

- Deepen knowledge of the topics by exploring what the situation is in both local and global spaces. Use real contexts, local and global, and locate subjects in the narrative of people and their society.
- Ask critical questions to provoke students' curiosity and develop their inquiry and critical thinking skills. Encourage students to think in terms of systems.
- Ensure that the student-centred approach is balanced by the community-centred approach.
- Encourage students to take action to address sustainability issues in, for and with their community.
- Model respect and caring for self, others and the environment in the classroom.
- Focus on values and attitudes for a peaceful, just and caring world.
- Use the 3Cs approach – (1) context, (2) content and (3) community connections.

In addition, especially from a SIDS perspective, ESD needs to focus on addressing students' issues of identity, agency, capabilities and resilience. "Vision, Values and Virtue", to use Miller's (2003) words, need to be central in teaching and learning for sustainable SIDS and a sustainable world.

6 REVISIONING ASSESSMENT IN EDUCATION FOR SUSTAINABLE DEVELOPMENT

TO FULFIL THE VISION OF A SUSTAINABLE WORLD, of thriving and flourishing societies, we need to position not only our teaching and learning for achieving that vision but also our forms of assessment. Assessments are after all a significant element of schooling. We need, therefore, to be mindful of the larger purpose of assessment – that of clarifying the readiness of individuals to acknowledge self as part of "the community of life". Their willingness to care, respect and protect both human and non-human lives needs to be demonstrated. We explore assessment then as part of teaching and learning that offers students a vision of a transformed life and world. Positioned here, assessment for ESD helps students to interact with their environment (in ways that are nurturing for both); elucidates their pathways through values clarification, critical, reflective and creative thinking; and enables them to move towards an integrated self and community.

The assessment of students must also be seen in relation to their schooling and how far that has enabled them to achieve a sense of self, capability, agency, of resilience for their community. We are only at the beginning of such radical ways of evaluating progress in schooling. For a start, we need to acknowledge the extent to which the present forms of assessment are separated from the "real world".

In the poem "Examination Centre", the poet Mervyn Morris (1992, 9) does this as he enlarges our perspective about our conventional forms of assessment. The poem highlights the vast gulf between the exam and "real" life. The exam is imaged as a kind of prison with the students represented as "sufferers / on edge". The poet details this suffering as he captures the reduction of the students and the enlarged power of the examiner, "the chief invigilator / gives the word / the fingered papers rustle". More important is the truth that the poet reveals – this is a world of fingers and paper, only a fragment of ourselves, the "real" world awaits. It is the world that is located beyond the walls of the examination centre. It is one in which

> trees bend and stretch
> and breathe
> winds, playful, tease

The nature images suggest freedom beyond the structures of human beings. And even as it is an idealized image, it makes no less real the way schooling and its forms of assessment are often barriers instead of paths to a liberated and harmonious world.

An alternative to this kind of "locked-in" structure of schooling is suggested in the poet's perspective of an education liberated by the questions it encourages and a vision of a transformed life:

> We're struggling here
> with questions
> and time
> and longing
> for a life we glimpse
> through dust
> clouding the panes

The poem alludes to the complex and too often unvoiced questions about life and another life in the deepest sense, questions that are many times ignored in classrooms and therefore absent in assessment rooms.

National assessments, that is, public examinations give us on a macro level the meaning of assessments. They have been understood as necessary for opportunities for employment and further studies (Heyneman 2009). However, a too narrow implementation of assessment as determined by the market and higher education has often led to the disconnect between education and real life, as illustrated in Morris's poem and discussed in chapter 1.

Some of these examinations have been largely that of summative assessments and managed by an external body (Griffith 2015). However, in the Caribbean in 1972, in mainly post-independent societies in the region, a regional body was established – the Caribbean Examinations Council (CXC). It is an examination body more aware and sensitive to regional needs and challenges than an international body. It is responsive to the Caribbean context and aspirations as Griffith (2015) emphasizes in his reflection on the history of this Caribbean examination body and the standard of these examinations. Griffith, in effect, points to the value of assessments as they connect with the real world of students and as they include the vision of a society.

The CXC has included both forms of assessments – summative as well as formative assessments. As such they reflect the purpose of assessments as assessment for learning; assessment about what is learned, assessment for application. Griffith's (2015) discussion of these is significant. Griffith highlights the importance of authentic assessments which formative assessments allow and argues that they provide opportunities for students to make the connection between learning and life. This should allow for the inclusion of a sustainability perspective. Critically reflecting on a few Caribbean Secondary Examination Certificate questions will allow us to understand more clearly what it means to have assessments for the development of sustainable societies. It will also make clear how assessments can embody a vision of a world that is just, peaceful, and respectful of the environment.

An emphasis on assessments that are connected to real life will focus on students applying knowledge in real-world situations. The value of an examination paper may thus be ascertained in terms of its emphasis on recall questions versus higher-order questions requiring some application. Yet too many examination questions are at the level of recall, for example, questions requiring students only to define, describe or explain. Moreover, some questions which require students to apply knowledge can be too textbook bound, and as a result, students fail to associate them with real-life or with the concept of a sustainable world.

The question taken from a food and nutrition regional examination paper is a good example of a question in which students are required to apply their subject knowledge to real-life situations. "Give 2 possible reasons why Sally no longer eats meats; Give 2 health benefits for Sally's choice; Plan an appropriate 2-course lunch meal for Sally." This is a good question.

However, this question could be more aligned to ESD if the local and/or global context were applied. Moreover, asking the students to plan a two-course lunch meal, which is outside the experiences of most of the children, makes the task too textbook-related and so unreal.

On the other hand, creating a brief narrative around this situation of the important topic of food and health and then questioning students on it would be more effective. Imagine giving Sally a particular context with details of the country, occupation, her past eating habits, her present improved eating habits as well as providing students with facts about food and health. These facts could come from World Bank data or country-specific data. Then students could be asked questions concerning the relation between Sally's eating and her health. Students could then be asked to plan two meals (instead of a two-course meal) that would be appropriate. Or if knowledge of a two-course lunch meal is being tested, the teacher could place it in a setting where this is the norm. More so, students could be given meal details and asked to comment on how healthy or not they are. With this approach, the question would help students focus on good health and well-being (SDG 3). The assessment would lead students to think about their community through applying the knowledge gained. This would further build on their learning to connect with the community. Table 3 makes this clearer.

In another paper, a mathematics test, students are given information about the minimum temperatures, in degrees Celsius, recorded in Country A for the first twenty days in a particular month. They are then asked to complete the frequency table using the information, determine the median temperature and calculate the mean temperature for the twenty days. Here students are applying knowledge learned. However, with a sustainability perspective, this subject-specific question could be adjusted to one that would have students also consider climate change and its impact.

Here are examples of content being evaluated with an emphasis on the context of sustainability.

Example 1 – Evaluating Content through Emphasis on Context

A mathematics exam question gives students a short narrative about two families and their use of water. Students are then asked to note patterns

Table 3. Contextualized Assessment

Questions asking learners to recall facts	Define "blanching"; "overnutrition"	Can easily be found on the internet
	Describe the following characters	Requires specific knowledge of the text
	Discuss the dramatic function of one of these characters	Requires knowledge of how characters are employed for purposes of plot, theme and so on
		Requires specific knowledge of the text
Questions asking learners to relate question to context	Give two possible reasons why Sally no longer eats meats	Requires some general knowledge/awareness of local and global social trends, as well as textual knowledge of the connection between eating meat and health
	Give two health benefits for Sally's choice	
	Plan appropriate two-course lunch meal for Sally	Requires knowledge of the text as well as cultural knowledge and how to apply that

and variables. Added to these specific algebra questions are two questions related to social justice. Here the sustainability vision of equity and water resources is integrated into the specific subject. What the examiner has done is to employ the subject to contribute to the sustainability vision. Students are thus being assessed for learning how to apply knowledge and specifically how to apply knowledge through clarification of values and connecting with their community.

1. Do you think it is right for some families to get very little water and for others to get lots and lots of water? Discuss this.
2. What pattern of water distribution would you want in your locality?

Write the pattern using variables. (Based on an extract from Wagner et al. 2017, 59.)

Example 2 – Evaluating Content through Emphasis on Context

A language question asks students to identify words or phrases used to praise or vilify an individual. They are then asked to analyse these phrases in terms of word choice; word order; tense, imagery and any other device used. Following this, they are asked to write a brief paragraph describing how reading these phrases made them feel and how they think it made the individual feel. Next, they are asked to examine how either praising or vilifying an individual can create a particular kind of community. This is followed by asking students to revise newspaper headlines in terms of the vision of a peaceful, just and caring world and to discuss briefly the process and the possible results.

In this assessment activity, teachers are examining word choices and other language devices. They are also assessing students' ability to write fluently and accurately in sentences, checking on language usage. Values clarification and critical thinking skills are also being included. Here the emphasis is on assessment for learning how to create a peaceful and just society as well as about what can retard or enhance the development of such a society. The question is responding to SDG 16, "promote just, peaceful and inclusive societies". Such forms of assessment are deliberately focusing on and creating the kind of world we want. Subject specifics should be tested within the larger framework of the world we live in and its future.

An ESD emphasizes real-world connections. Assessments that centre on these connections and the application of what has been learned are aligned with the goals of ESD. Carless (2017) in his study of students' experiences of assessment for learning points out that students reacted enthusiastically to assessments that were relevant to real-world applications of the discipline. An example that he gave was of law students producing a "reflective media diary about legal cases reported in the media as well as an assessed report of a self-organized visit to a Labour Tribunal" (Carless 2017, 5). The assessment was valued because it was closely related to the daily practice of law.

The real-world connection can be made even more meaningful if contextualized by local issues and aspirations. In SIDS where many people may experience marginalization, assessments that place value on the individual student contribute to reversing such marginalization. School-based assessment, like those organized by CXC, reflects a strong awareness of the aspirations of such individuals and regions. Ensuring that the students' examination profile is not limited to the single examination paper, that every attention is paid to students' continuous learning and assessment being part of the students' learning, indicates an examination that aims to be fair, just and inclusive. Underpinning this is the idea of equity, of an acknowledgement that the social and economic context of inequality has to be addressed at some level. Students' diverse capabilities and interests are given space to grow in that approach to assessment.

The focus here has been on CXC. Cases have been used to illustrate what obtains and what more is needed in assessments for the development of a people, conscious of the future being created.

Assessments informed by a global view of human aspirations and by a worldview of sustainability shaped by the local or regional cultural, socioeconomic, and ecological landscape will see more attention being paid to assessments employed as a tool for student development. In this case, students' self-development means more than the acquisition of knowledge and skills: it means being positively responsive to the community, being resilient and able to overcome the hurdles in a developing nation state, being caring and respectful of self, and engaging in actions for the transformation of the community.

Such assessments place value on the students. This is reflected also in acknowledgements of their capability. So they are given opportunities to co-create their assessments with their teachers. That kind of assessment would allow students to identify their achievement expectations and to monitor their progress in partnership with their teacher (Stiggins 2005). Incorporating self and peer assessment would also validate students. Spiller (2012) emphasizes the importance of this kind of assessment. She points out that the value of learners in the constructivist classroom is recognized as they are treated as co-creators of knowledge. She argues therefore that, similarly, learners need to be co-creators of feedback for their learning. She further alerts us to how the learners' development can be severely limited if the teacher holds all the power and makes all the assessment choices.

Even though self and peer assessment can enhance the student's sense of self, it is not widely practiced, even at the tertiary level. Such forms of assessment can pose a wide range of challenges. Notwithstanding these, Spiller (2012) observes that students receiving feedback from their peers can get a wider range of ideas about their work to promote their development and improvement.

Of particular importance is assessment based on group work or participation. Education for sustainability encourages collaboration and engagement of students. The value of cooperation, of recognizing one's place alongside others as well as active engagement in the "learning" community is essential to students' learning to appreciate the community of life. These values underpin their learning to live together and learning to transform themselves and society. These forms of assessments are often challenging, however. Carless (2017) indicates that students find that assessing participation helps to keep them engaged despite its subjective nature and the vagueness of criteria for that form of assessment.

Similarly, the advantages of group work assessment are generally acknowledged by students. Such assessments prepare them to work with others, provide peer support, build cooperation and trust. Yet as Carless's (2017) study reveals, students experience many difficulties with forms of assessment that are related to the process of teamwork and the final product. An example of this was the irresponsible behaviour of some team members, which in turn led to undue responsibility placed on one member. He asserts, however, that these challenges can be effectively met and identifies several strategies to deal with these including interim reports and ongoing feedback.

In classrooms where the *vision* for a sustainable world is embedded, we know that each action, each task including the assessment is shaped around the achievement of this vision. The teacher with a sustainability worldview will consider assessment in terms of the bigger picture, the well-being of our world. Moreover, as Bramwell-Lalor (2019) asserts, an ESD with its emphasis on attitudes and values, action-oriented learning, on critical thinking skills requires assessment forms that fully respond to these areas. She suggests that alternative assessment strategies that focus on assessment for learning should include case studies, portfolios, projects, work- or industry-based tasks, reflective journals and drama. She acknowledges that values, attitudes and behaviours are affective or dispositional learning outcomes and difficult to measure. Yet she posits that there are means to do this which include observation and carefully drawn rubrics that set out the criteria for quantitative grades.

The following basic questions will help us to determine the most appropriate forms of assessment: What are we assessing? Why are we assessing this? How do we assess this?

Let us consider these in turn: What are we assessing? Too often the emphasis has been on assessing content knowledge. No doubt, this is important. Yet with easy access to knowledge via the Internet, the emphasis need not be placed here. Recalling the 3Cs we realize how important the context for content learning is – students need to know their local as well as global context; they need to know the SDGs, which together spell out the vision for transforming our world; they need to know the values that are underpinning these goals; and they need to have the critical skills to work for achieving them.

If the emphasis is placed on context for content as discussed, the assessment would, therefore, be on investigating, critically reflecting on, analysing students' local and global community, to address the challenges they face. The particularity of the subject content would be framed by this context.

Moreover, in testing content, it is more important to assess students' skills to analyse content. This will include students knowing how to determine bias and perspective, to understand the significance of that content and how to use that content to transform themselves as well as their communities. Content is easily accessible. Our assessment of students should then focus on the development of thinking skills, on values creation and clarification as well as on actions and connections to the community.

Traditionally, assessments have often been done as a way to reward the good student, that is, the student who has worked hard, has studied the content and can regurgitate well what has been taught; in effect, the student who has met the stated as well as hidden criteria. At the core, it separates the supposedly lazy and incompetent students from the ones who are diligent and competent. It marks those who should advance. In reality, it subtly sets competition in motion and works towards exclusion. Too often, the assessment does not take into account different styles of learning and different ways of responding to being tested.

ASSESSMENT FOR LEARNING TO LIVE WELL IN COMMUNITY

Students bring knowledge from their community. Their community teaches and learns from them. Education that enables students to interact with their community, to learn in, for and with their community is an education that can transform our societies into sustainable ones. To assess this kind of education, we want to evaluate skills and knowledge in action, that is, applied knowledge. Additionally, we want assessment to continue to be part of students' learning. A key goal here is to enable students to be reflective and to be able to assess themselves.

It is within this context that we will explore a highly effective way of assessing students: the community action project. This form of assessment bears several similarities to field trips, service learning and action projects in general. These forms of assessment have often been seen as less rigorous, less demanding than the paper and pen tests. Yet such real-world examinations can be as or more rigorous than the conventional forms, and in addition far more effective in transforming our world. Engaging in community action projects is a way of moving from a too-narrow focus on individual achievement and self-interest to one of community transformation. The project acknowledges that students need to be connected to the community so that they can see its significance and learn to care for and respect it. The assessment focuses, therefore, on the community as well as individual transformation.

Let us examine this case study of assessment through a community action project. This is an assessment for learning as well as an evaluation of students' actions for addressing sustainability concerns in their community. It is also continuous as the assessment takes place over some time. Students are given these guidelines and asked to respond to the following questions.

A. Preparation for the Project

1. Initial feelings about carrying out a project
   - How do I feel about having to do a project?
   - Why do I feel this way?
2. Selecting a project
   - What problems am I very concerned about?
   - What problems do I think that I can best tackle?

– What will I need to tackle these problems?

– Which one will I select?

– Why?

3. Making an action plan

– Define exactly what the problem is.

– Decide exactly what you want to do – measurable objectives.

– List steps you will have to take to make it happen.

– Prepare a timeline.

B. Implementing the Project

1. Begin. Put your plan into action. Implement. Critically reflect.

– Critically reflect on your actions daily/weekly. Record your observations and your feelings.

– What was supposed to happen?

– What happened?

– What were the positive and negative factors?

– How do I move forward?

2. Identifying, critically reflecting on what was done and learned.

– What did you achieve? (a) What did the participants experience? (b) What did you and they accomplish?

– What could have gone better? What happened to stop you from achieving more? How can you ensure that future work will go better?

– How satisfied do you feel about the way it went? How would you rate your satisfaction level on a scale of 1 to 10? What made or would have made it a "perfect 10" for you?

– How has your project helped to create a better community?

Students are expected to follow this and to create a reflective log on their actions, observations and thoughts about the project. They are assessed based on the following:

• Selection and planning of project

• Process of implementation

• Achievement of project idea

There are important similarities and differences between this and CXC's school-based project report, which includes "a statement of the problem, reasons for selecting the area of research, method of investigation, procedures for data collection, data analysis and interpretation, statement of findings, and recommendations based on the findings" (Griffith 2015, 63). The community action project includes these elements. However, it is focused on the community and action in the community. The assessment also aims at developing and "testing" critical and reflective skills.

This project assessment also reflects many of the criteria that CXC lists: concepts, knowledge, skills and competencies (Griffith 2015). In addition, the community action project assessment emphasizes "attitudes and values" – a criterion that we see identified in the Office Administration syllabus which is to "help students appreciate the wide range of attitudes, attributes and behaviours necessary for success and advancement in the world of work". Ironically, it is a criterion missing in the overall profile grades for the Caribbean Secondary Examination Certificate. The focus here is on key concepts, knowledge, skills and competencies.

On the other hand, an ESD-infused examination process, using a mix of traditional assessment methods and more reflective and performance-based approaches, such as self-assessment and peer assessment, enables educators to capture learners' insights regarding their personal transformation, their growing capacity for critical inquiry and engagement and civic agency, among others (Leicht, Heiss and Byun 2018). In other words, the emphasis is on real-world assessment. An action-based assessment involves critical and reflective thinking and is in the final analysis transformative of self and society.

A culture shift is thus required. Bramwell-Lalor's (2019) assertion that we need to move beyond the traditional individualistic and competitive forms of assessment to one that encompasses the affective, including that of cooperation and collaboration is timely. The paradigmatic shift in teaching and learning for sustainable development begs for comparative forms of assessment.

Assessments cannot be just for the sake of assessments, for the market or further studies if we acknowledge the importance of ESD. Assessments need to cater to the market requirements and further studies, yet more important is assessment for the transformation of the individual and the local and global society. The UNESCO learning pillars and the list of ESD competencies (Leicht, Heiss and Byun 2018; UNECE 2012) need, therefore, to be considered as guides for assessments.

In the Caribbean, the drop-out rate from schools is disconcertingly high for males, and as a result, male overall enrolment in higher education institutions is significantly lower than females. In light of this situation, we suggest that there is a need for regional research on the role of assessments in retaining or contributing to the high dropout rate of males in educational institutions. The questions are whether assessments need to be more deeply rooted in respect for the learner and their place, more attuned to identifying the capabilities of learners for transforming their communities and place more emphasis on the values they hold than on ready-made textbook answers.

Changing the way we do assessments would support the transformation being advocated towards a new education paradigm, one centred on equity, respect and stewardship of the earth.

7 | EXEMPLARS OF EDUCATION FOR SUSTAINABLE DEVELOPMENT PROCESSES AND PRACTICES

THE CONCEPTS OF SUSTAINABLE DEVELOPMENT and ESD have been explored across the globe. UNESCO, through its various forums and publications, has mediated these discussions and played a major role in defining and clarifying these terms to build a common understanding. Notwithstanding, these concepts have to be interpreted and understood in local terms. The UNESCO ESD Sourcebook (2012) has pointed out that sustainable development has to be relevant to local contexts. The same obtains for ESD.

It is against this background that recent research on ESD was conducted in Jamaica by the authors as previously outlined. Using a quantitative and qualitative approach, six academics in the quantitative and thirteen academics in the qualitative phases in a tertiary institution participated in a survey and focus group discussions. The research sought to find out these lecturers' understanding of sustainable development and ESD as well as their practice of ESD. The findings are significant. Locally grounded, they add substantially to the literature on twenty-first-century quality education and ESD. The findings also indicate limitations that can be addressed through the exploration of ESD understandings and practices on a global level. The importance of intertwining local understandings and practices with global ones becomes clear.

These findings inform this chapter. Additionally, this chapter examines case studies illustrating various ESD processes and practices. Specifically, these case studies include exemplars of the infusion of ESD; of a university-led community project framed by ESD; and a whole school approach to ESD.

Summary of Findings

Lecturers' Understanding of the Concept of Sustainable Development

All lecturers shared a common understanding of sustainable development. They conceptualized it as social and economic progress that included environmental conservation and equitable human development. Social justice and equity were key elements. Additionally, they spoke about sustainable development as one that leads to "a good quality of life" and one that has future generations in mind. The destruction of the environment and the development of nuclear weapons were seen as retrogressive elements. Their definitions of sustainable development were, in fact, consonant with the UNESCO definition, which states that sustainability is a paradigm that allows for futures-oriented thinking in which environmental, social, economic and cultural considerations are balanced as development and improved quality of life are pursued (UNESCO 2012).

An interesting perspective that the lecturers contributed was the idea of "sufficiency"; a sustainable society is one in which everyone has enough. They also made the significant point that for the concept to be accepted, it must be part of the common mindset of people. This could be achieved, as one lecturer noted, if people were able to see the "virtue and value" of sustainability. Expanding on this, another lecturer noted that if people saw themselves as benefiting from this view of and rollout of development, then this idea would gain widespread acceptance.

However, they found the idealized way in which the concept was defined and elaborated on in the SDGs problematic. For them, the goals set in their aspirational form made their attainment appear unrealistic and unachievable.

Lecturers' Understanding of Quality Twenty-First-Century Education

Lecturers saw learning to care for self, others and the environment as core to quality education. They felt that the current practice of treating the learning of values as part of the so-called hidden curriculum, as something to be done indirectly, needed to be changed. As one lecturer expressed it, "so-called hidden curriculum stuff should be more overt and maybe not so hidden again". A number of the lecturers elaborated on this idea of values education; they felt that it should also include helping students to develop self-love and self-awareness. This self-awareness would include knowledge of their significance to society and a recognition that society needs their unique contribution. Moreover, it was suggested that a lack of self-love was in part responsible for many of the sustainability problems facing the world today.

The development of skills was also identified as crucial to quality education. Critical thinking skills were highlighted. Lecturers noted that there has to be a shift away from simply giving students a particular body of knowledge, as knowledge was dynamic and access to knowledge was relatively easy. They stated emphatically that what students need to learn is how to determine the quality of the knowledge, how to analyse and apply it. The emphasis on passing examinations, on regurgitating content presented in the classroom, needed to be changed. One lecturer explained that the focus on passing examinations has led to many students having a tunnel vision regarding their learning, on wanting to focus only on what is going to be tested. Other skills that were identified as important included learning to be resilient and adaptable.

A novel finding was that lecturers wanted students to have a visioning mind. This was closely aligned with the discussion on self-care and self-love. It was pointed out that students who have a vision of themselves as succeeding, who set goals, who think about the future are more likely to succeed in their endeavours than those who do not. Mindful that some students live with social and financially challenging circumstances, lecturers spoke to the importance of students dreaming and envisioning the realization of their potential.

Quality education was in effect conceptualized as one that "allows people to sustain themselves, to live well among each other and engage in practices that will lead to better societies". Or as expressed by another lecturer, "to prepare students to function efficiently, effectively and harmoniously in the world". And though the idea of caring for the environment was not explicitly stated and there was the shadow of an anthropocentric viewpoint, the lecturers clearly conceived a harmonious world and a better society as one that includes the entire community of life.

In further exploring the concept of quality education, lecturers high-lighted the importance of teachers' belief in their students. They spoke to quality education as one in which teachers actively care for and respect their students and are focused on their transformation. Such teachers can reflect a positive self-image to their students, which is foundational for their students' developing care for others and the environment.

Lecturers' Practices for Quality Education for ESD

Translating the vision of a sustainable society into classroom practice is challenging. The lecturers interviewed spoke to specific ways in which they integrated their vision and their concept of a transformed society. It was clear that, on one level, lecturers enacted their beliefs in terms of their rela-tionships and interactions with their students. On another level, they were engaged in specific practices and activities that reflected an attunement to sustainability. They also spoke of the challenges they faced as they attempted to align their sustainability vision with their classroom practices.

These interactions were marked by ensuring that their classrooms were inclusive. One lecturer expressed it this way, "I'm going to pull everyone in." Lecturers, therefore, aimed for the engagement of all students. They affirmed the importance of students' voices. One lecturer illustrated this by pointing to the centrality of students' voices in her research as well as in her classroom practice. Another lecturer pointed to his acknowledgement of the uniqueness of the contribution of each student as he created space for each student to lead. Contrary to much of the literature on "Leadership", which speaks to leaders and followers, his belief that everyone is a leader, underpinned his approach. The inclusive approach here is broad-based, including not only race, gender and class but also the "fingerprint", the "I am" of each person, their uniqueness. Believing that each one holds a key to creating a better society, lecturers aimed at welcoming students' uniqueness and differences.

Paralleling this approach was that of lecturers actively caring and re-specting each student. Lecturers spoke to creating safe classroom spaces. By using humour, thus making lessons also fun, students could feel at ease. A comfortable space in which students could express their lack of knowledge or limited abilities was also created. In this way, their limitations could be addressed in caring and respectful ways. Important too was lecturers' acknowledging their students' potential and valuing their contribution; this they affirmed made students feel respected. Such acknowledgement was expressed in lecturers encouraging their students to be producers and not mere consumers, as in the example cited by one lecturer who recalled how she engaged students in making their own videos instead of merely acquiring videos. The importance of this cannot be overstated especially for countries labelled "developing", "third world" or "underdeveloped".

ESD incorporates knowing about, analysing and addressing sustainable development issues. Ensuring that real issues are explored and attended to is a given for a teacher in an ESD-infused classroom. These lecturers affirmed the importance of connecting their lectures to real life. They did this in several ways. One way was broadening the context of their curriculum to include current issues. One individual, for example, discussed how he facilitated students' inquiry into some of the key sustainable development issues in the region and provided opportunities for them to arrive at "scientific answers". Drawing on scientists, like Dr Thomas Lecky, who had made significant discoveries for improving agriculture in the region, he encouraged students to focus on scientific research that would help to alleviate poverty, economic problems, among other sustainability ones. The lecturers named this approach as "going beyond the subject".

There are, however, some challenges to enacting a curriculum reoriented to sustainability. Lecturers identified the challenge of centring values. Educating for respect, for care has often been on the margins of the curriculum even as their importance is recognized. Consistently making this a focal point of lessons was seen as problematic. In addition, environmental issues, though incorporated, were treated tangentially. To include issues, absent in the curriculum or syllabus was seen as no easy task.

Ironically, the term "ESD" was not used by the lecturers to describe what they were doing, yet they had a sustainability perspective and were using an ESD approach in their classrooms. This has implications for how curriculum and teachers' practice can be reoriented for sustainability. The lecturers, however, in identifying their challenges spoke to the need for further understanding of how to infuse sustainability in their teaching in a consistent way; how to ensure the values they want their students to treasure become core in their practice; how to make connections between classroom and community and encourage students to learn in, with and for a sustainable community, a sustainable society.

The findings of the research on teachers which were discussed highlight some of the achievements of lecturers with a sustainability perspective and the insights they offer for ESD. The findings also reveal some of the gaps that a fuller understanding of ESD can meet. The following case studies will show various ways of doing so and of engaging more fully with ESD.

The case studies were selected based on the expressed needs of the lecturers interviewed as well as the gaps identified in the literature. The case studies of (1) infusion in a university course and (2) into textbooks provide concrete examples of exemplary approaches to incorporating ESD, which have emerged from the field. The textbook project is one of the few such projects globally. Moreover, the text which emerged was used to engage teacher-writers at the primary and secondary level to produce textbooks with ESD infused. The other case study, that of a working group for ESD at a university, illustrates how a whole-institution approach for ESD may begin within a school of education. A fourth case study seeks to highlight peace education, an ESD-related education, in action through a school culture change methodological approach. Another case study, the master of education in ESD, shows how ESD can be a discrete subject and yet one that invites transdisciplinary work.

CASE STUDY 1: LEARNING TO INFUSE ESD INTO A UNIVERSITY COURSE – CHANGING CULTURES, CHANGING SCHOOLS

This course aims to help pre- and in-service teachers understand the change process so that they could become effective change agents. Course participants analyse the nature of school culture and its relation to the wider culture. They also examine the role of various stakeholders (teachers, students, principals, among others) in shaping school culture. Specifically, participants explore how they and their students can transform school culture.

We now look at the infusion of ESD into this course using the 3Cs format: context, content and community connections. That is, (1) the concept of sustainable development and the vision of sustainable schools was acknowledged as the context for the teaching of this course, and so there was a focus on transforming society; (2) the content of the course was blended with the content for sustainable development – its issues, values; and (3) the course engaged students in connecting with the community, learning in, with and for the community.

We now elaborate on this further. With the concept of sustainable development as the context for the course, the teaching and learning of the course involved specific kinds of activities. These included (1) visioning for a sustainable society. This was introduced in several ways: students were asked to complete mapping of local sustainability issues, noting their social, economic and environmental dimensions; students were also asked to engage in focused school and community observations. (2) There were lectures and discussions on the concept of sustainability, its varied definitions and the background leading to the development of the concept; there was also a reflection on UNESCO documents on ESD, various texts on ESD, the Millennium Development Goals and the SDGs.

We also tried, from the start of the course, to create a classroom environment based on respect and care for self and others, mindful of the need to model the essence of sustainability – that of caring and respecting self and others.

The course included the topics understanding school cultures, changing school cultures, school reforms and exemplary schools, and it was framed by the concept and practice of sustainability. The approach was that of making real-world connections, so Ministry of Education officers, principals and teachers engaged in school culture change shared their experiences and data in class presentations. Other activities included the exploration of popular culture in terms of sustainable development issues. These included popular songs, cultural icons, local proverbs, among others. Reflections on schools, locally and globally involved in changing schools for sustainability were also incorporated. International Eco-Schools programmes, schools' environmental programmes, the Change from Within programme (a Jamaican peace programme) were also examined. As students studied change processes, the complexities and theories about school culture and change, they learned how these were grounded in social, economic and environmental concerns. Issues of violence, poverty, justice, climate change, environmental degradation, for example, and their relation to school culture informed the course content.

The *connection* to the real world was made throughout the entire course as indicated in the discussion on concept and content. However, it was made more directly as students engaged in action projects in their schools to transform the culture into one that was more peaceful, caring and environmentally aware. Students were thus allowed to apply and deepen their knowledge of sustainability and cultural change processes as they connected what was being done in the classroom to that of the school community.

Course delivery was student-centred and action-oriented, comprising lectures, video presentations, music, group and individual presentations as well as community action projects.

The assessment of the course was also in keeping with the pedagogical orientation. They were "varied, ranging from theoretical papers exploring ESD as a global reform effort and its local relevance to the design of a sustainable school to the development and initiation of an action plan within students' school and institutional setting aimed at changing a negative aspect of their school's culture" (Ferguson and Bramwell-Lalor 2018, 90).

Tables 4 and 5 highlight examples of the projects undertaken and students' reflections on their role as change agents.

Table 4. Examples of School Culture Change Projects

Aspect of School Culture Identified for Change	Components of Action Plan Utilizing an Aspect of Jamaican Culture to Initiate Change
Fighting, violence	Football – initiation of a "Get Along League"; incorporation of "football rules" into regular classroom activities, for example, red card if fight occurs
Littering, waste management	Music – creation of action songs about proper garbage disposal
Lack of respect, disrespectful behaviour	Music – playing of songs about respect during school devotions; organization of a "respect" song competition
Parental involvement	Healthy food – hosting of parental workshops and the serving of meals; hosting of healthy meal demonstrations; organization of a parent-child cook-off competition

Source: Ferguson and Bramwell-Lalor 2018.

Table 5. Students' Reflections on Their Experiences as Change Agents and Their Engagement with Education for Sustainable Development

"I found the experience of being a change agent to be a rewarding one. It allowed me to recognize that there were indeed others who also recognized the need for change and I did not feel as if I were alone swimming against the tide. I also learned that if there is indeed to be change one cannot sit by complaining about the need for change but one has to actually be that change. Change occurs through action and not through idle talk and constant complaining."

"Over the several weeks of engaging in the different class activities, and being challenged to write my assignment papers, I have been completely matured in my thought process and my sense of responsibility. I am now fully aware of my responsibility as a sustainable agent. In order for there to be continued growth within the education system and the world at large I will have to take the responsibility of doing what I can so that the next generation to come will have a future and a place to live and practice their craft. I now know that sustainable development is not a project of central government, but each of us as individuals has a duty to help sustain the environment for the future users."

"Embarking on this journey was therapeutic for me as I realized that this was an avenue to baptize myself with the art of forgiveness. So, while I was being an agent of change for persons in my department, I was being an agent of change for myself."

"As a change agent, I realized that buy-in was critical to what needs to be achieved and if it was to meet the sustainability test. Sustainability is meeting the needs of the present generation…while not compromising the ability of the future generations to meet their needs. I quickly realized that this sustainability test must be achieved if there is going to be any true change."

Source: Ferguson and Bramwell-Lalor 2018.

Case Study 2: The UNESCO Mahatma Gandhi Institute of Education for Peace Textbooks for Sustainable Development – A Guide to Embedding

In the UNESCO Mahatma Gandhi Institute of Education for Peace and Sustainable Development (UNESCO MGIEP) textbook project, we also have another example of how ESD can be infused or embedded into the curriculum. In this instance, it is exemplified in textbooks. The process that will be discussed here can be used also with teaching the subject.

In 2016, twenty-nine experts (researchers and practitioners of ESD) met in Bangalore, India, to discuss how to embed ESD into mathematics, science, geography and language (English) textbooks. These subjects were considered core and could provide the template for others. From this group of twenty-nine, four lead authors were selected to work along with contributing authors to write the guide. Two key questions shaped the approach:

1. What does your subject contribute to sustainable development, to a sustainable world?
2. What are the tools and processes that can be used to embed ESD in your subject?

The questions reflected the notion that each subject has something to contribute to a sustainable society. Infusion or embedding ESD into each subject was, therefore, a stronger structure than simply adding ESD as another subject to the curriculum (figure 4).

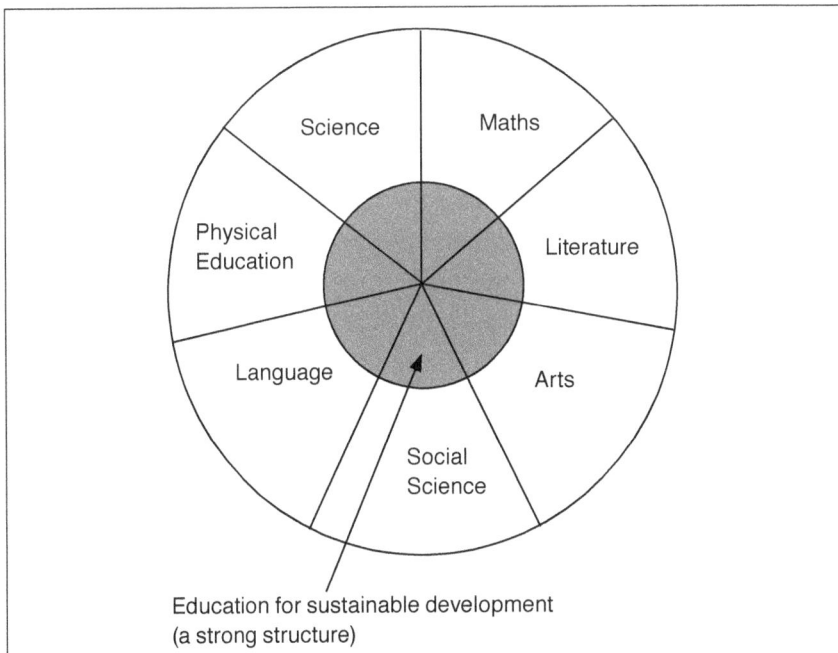

Figure 4. Education for sustainable development as a multidisciplinary subject

The special contribution that each subject can make to a healthy and flourishing world was identified. It was also agreed that to reorient textbooks to address directly sustainable development, we needed to look at content and pedagogy. Content included cross-cutting sustainable development issues such as climate change, peace and social justice. The pedagogical approach taken included content presented as more than the simple transmission of information but more that of connecting knowledge to real-life contexts, making it concrete and engaging students to respond critically to its complexity.

The emphasis shifted from students' acquisition of knowledge to their making sense of knowledge and applying it to resolve sustainability concerns. Textbooks were also envisaged as helping students to see knowledge, not as something fixed but as something developing and complex. The learning of critical thinking skills needed, therefore, to be emphasized. Complementing this was the attention to values.

These textbooks were expected to engage students intellectually and emotionally in sustainable development and to make sustainable development issues and topics matter to students. The guide led to the UNESCO MGIEP Sikkim Textbook Project in which the State Council of Educational Research and Training in Sikkim and UNESCO MGIEP, Ajim Premji University, Bangalore, textbook writers and the lead writers for the guide collaborated to produce textbooks for students in grades 1 through 5. The textbooks produced were for maths, environmental studies and English. We will now focus on how the authors embedded ESD in mathematics.

The mathematics group of authors saw mathematical actions of counting, measuring and locating as connected to people and their environments. To reorient for sustainable development would mean exploring how such actions could be used to promote a clear understanding of complex situations, real-life situations and advance the sustainability vision. They identified, for example, how such mathematical tools could help students learn to work out the balance between short- and long-term needs and how they could work out future availability of resources. A specific example was that of students learning how farmers can reduce waste and maximize their profits if they can successfully predict how much of their goods could be sold. Learning about accurate modelling – a mathematical process – could help with food security issues and having meaningful work.

They linked the basic functions of Maths, the use of data and statistics, and Geometry to various topics such as climate data and climate change; development of street traffic, traffic fatalities and exhaust emissions in different countries over time; interest and repayment for private and public loans, water demands, water scarcity; generation and consumption of energy. In essence, the focus was on identifying the mathematics involved in sustainability issues. The mathematics group summarized their approach to embedding ESD in mathematics textbooks:

> It is important for mathematics textbooks to show examples of how mathematics can be used to support SDGs, including disaster risk reduction. In addition to examples that help students to visualize injustice and unsustainable practices, examples of disasters – when people's best efforts go horribly wrong – help students to plan ways to address these challenges. It is also important to write the materials in a way that expects and instructs the students to interact with each other to solve complex problems. This teaches them to listen to other people, develop respect for other's viewpoints and to make mathematical choices that most responsibly address the complex problems our communities face. (Wagner et al. 2017, 50)

CASE STUDY 3: THE ESD WORKING GROUP

The ESD working group within the School of Education at the UWI was formed by a small core group of teacher educators, all from different specializations but with an interest in and commitment to ESD. Currently, the working group has ten members who also receive support and advisement from past retirees who are still active in the field. Over the years, the working group has been involved in the following:

- Course and programme development: Members have worked to develop courses with an ESD focus, such as the Literature and Education for Sustainable Development course. Additionally, there have been efforts to infuse ESD into courses within the members' various specialisations. As will be discussed below, members of the working group also developed an MEd programme in ESD.

- Capacity-building: Members have sought to build the capacity of educators nationally (in Jamaica) and within the wider Caribbean. For example, members have carried out ESD workshops for in-service teachers in countries such as Guyana in 2015. In addition to work with teachers and other educators, in-house capacity-building is delivered through staff seminars focused on areas such as the concepts of sustainable development and ESD, and how to infuse ESD.
- Public awareness and outreach: Through public lectures, panel discussions, poster displays and workshops, members have worked to raise awareness among the wider university community and public of ESD. These activities have taken place locally and internationally. Examples include a public lecture on forest land, sustainability and bird conservation in 2016, and a panel discussion on ESD teaching and learning with the future in mind at the International Council on Education for Teaching Conference in 2016.
- Research and publications: Research on different facets of ESD is carried out by group members in areas such as teacher education, infusion of ESD, CCESD, peace education and SDG 4. This research is shared through both conference presentations and publications. The research of the working group emerges from questions related to the teaching and learning experience. Many of these questions related to the "how" of ESD infusion. How do we infuse ESD into our teaching as a first step towards the institutionalization of ESD in the wider School of Education culture at the UWI? How do we make the process more conscious and deliberate? How do we make it an ongoing aspect of our teaching?

The majority of the current ESD working group members are relatively new members of staff who have been grappling with the same core question as to "how" to infuse ESD into their teaching. Based on this, over the 2018/19 academic year, the group undertook a collaborative action research project to infuse ESD into selected undergraduate or postgraduate courses (Roofe et al. 2021).

Before this process, in-house capacity-building of ESD working group members and the wider School of Education staff took place through several seminars on sustainable development, ESD and infusion. These were led by both staff members as well as colleagues from the Institute for Sustainable Development at the UWI and served to address issues surrounding the lack of understanding and ambiguity with the concepts of sustainable development and ESD. Additionally, as part of the process, members of the working group (new and retired) worked together to create a short video on ESD that could be utilized as a common starting point for members as well as students in the classes selected to be part of the infusion effort.

A detailed discussion of the collaborative effort is chronicled (Roofe et al. 2021); however, what can be shared here is that collaborative and collegial support was critical concerning the process. This suggests that efforts at infusion must benefit from the interdisciplinary dialogue, reflection and collaboration that characterizes ESD itself.

Case Study 4: The Change from Within Programme

As noted previously, values and attitudes are foundational for ESD. The need for social and moral character development in society was noted by one of the former vice-chancellors of the UWI, Sir Philip Sherlock. Troubled by what he realized was growing violence and indiscipline in schools, the Change from Within programme was born in 1992 out of Sherlock's mandate to a group of educators and social scientists to explore this phenomenon in greater detail and the possible response that education could offer to address the issue. This core team focused on four schools that were experiencing qualitative changes in their schools in areas of staff and student relations, self-esteem and self-image, decreased conflict and violence, and improvements in academics.

Over two decades later, the programme is now being implemented under the umbrella of ESD and Peace Education, with a continued focus on mentorship and coaching, leadership development, capacity-building and shared decision-making among all school stakeholders. Thus, the idea is not to try to address violence and indiscipline directly or solely but to instead try to engender institutional cultural change and to examine some of the wider issues that contribute to indiscipline, conflict and/or violence within schools. This is significant given Down's (2015b) proposition that schools within the Caribbean need to be recultured to align with and support the principles of sustainability, which includes of course peace and non-violence as one of these key principles. Some of the key areas of work in recent years have included the following:

- Circle of Friends: The Circle of Friends is an informal leadership development and support network, originally focused on school principals but since expanded to include various school stakeholders exhibiting leadership potential such as vice-principals, guidance counsellors and head teachers. Through the monthly meetings of the Circle of Friends, individuals share, discuss and reflect on various strategies and best practices for addressing violence and indiscipline in their school environments. Research carried out on the programme has highlighted the Circle of Friends as one of the most meaningful aspects of the programme (Down, Lambert and McPherson-Kerr 2005) and explored its significance in enhancing leadership capabilities to shape school cultures that promote peace, respect and self-esteem among the various stakeholders of schools (Ferguson, Samuels and Gordon 2018). Leadership has been critical in vision-setting, innovation and shared decision-making and collaboration to initiate and undertake school culture change (Chevannes 2005; Ferguson, Samuels and Gordon 2018; Ferguson et al. 2020).
- Training and capacity-building: Over the decades that the programme has been implemented, various capacity-building initiatives have been organized and delivered to principals/vice-principals, guidance counsellors, teachers, students and parents in areas such as health, money management, conflict management, parenting, child development, interpersonal relationships, the use of innovative pedagogies and ESD (Chevannes 2005; Ferguson 2017). These training initiatives serve to foster the various learning pillars in individuals such as the "learning to know", "learning to do", and "learning to transform oneself and society" (Ferguson 2016).
- Restorative justice: As part of the efforts to reshape and transform school cultures, various means of addressing conflicts are shared as alternatives to violence. One of these is the notion of the restorative justice circle or trust circles as sometimes used by the CFW programme team members. Utilizing the circles offers schools a way to address conflicts peacefully,

among staff, students and parents, and works to support the ESD pillars of learning and other ESD principles. As stated by Ferguson and Chevannes (2018, 61), "restorative justice fosters and allows participants to consider wider ESD and GCED values, such as justice, equity, respect and dignity. Circle members develop social skills and communication skills as they engage in dialogue, listening, negotiation and more. The circles also foster community connections; when one member of the school community suffers, all members suffer, thus emphasizing and enhancing compassion, empathy and care."

• Coaching: The use of coaching is a new element of the programme undertaken by the CFW's master coach with students identified as being at-risk in some form. The coach works with students individually (and sometimes in groups) to help them focus on goal-setting, communication, team-building and conflict resolution all as a means to help students in envisioning alternative futures and alternatives to violence (Ferguson 2019a).

Additionally, it is important to note that through the participatory action research process, in which change is driven by school stakeholders and involves a process of reflection and dialogue (Ferguson 2019c), individual attitudes and values are subjected to introspection. Additionally, the idea of "social affirmation", in which self, others, communities and groups are valued, affirmed and celebrated, is a significant element of the programme (Down 2019). The programme team supports the different activities of the schools through post-workshop/capacity-building event visits, emphasis on a train-the-trainers approach to support sustainability and research. Foundational to the programme's success is that of the programme having a strong moral purpose, a strong belief that positive change is possible and that peace is attainable. With a common vision and a deep commitment to the creation of a peaceful, just and sustainable world, the implementers can nurture feelings of hope – an essential element for transformation (Down and Down 2018). Indeed, modelling the values and beliefs consistent with ESD is something that the programme team strives to do in their interactions with the schools.

Case Study 5: MEd in ESD Programme

ESD working group members voiced several ideas about the type of society and the changes that are needed in the focus group sessions that formed phase two of our research, some of which we have already mentioned. These ideas included emphases on: values and attitudes, humane ways of being and living, and holistic human development. The master of education degree in education for sustainable development, global citizenship and peace responds to some of these needs and imperatives in the Caribbean. The programme was developed by the School of Education at the UWI Mona campus in Jamaica and commenced with its first cohort in the 2019/20 academic year. The programme is comprised of a series of core courses focused on EE and ESD, climate change, violence prevention and citizenship. These courses are taken alongside track courses (for those interested in formal or non-formal ESD) and research courses.

Course assignments are comprised of authentic and non-traditional assessments such as action projects and reflective pieces, alongside traditional assessments such as final examinations. Through engagement with the course material and undertaking of the assessments, students are provoked to critically reflect and interrogate individual underlying values and attitudes, and behaviour patterns, and how they contribute or do not contribute to a sustainable society. Additionally, they interrogate these ideas concerning their existence as well as their teaching and interactions with those in their schools and their communities. For instance, after engaging with some readings on ESD and traditional schooling in the ESD theories course, one student, in her reflective piece, wrote:

> I am challenged to inculcate in my students an attitude that takes them from just knowing the theory but applying the information to their everyday life. It has forced me to expand my understanding of environmental education from just the natural environment to encompass the built and social environment and to also advocate for this environment. I was also challenged by the reminder that I'm a part of the community and if I make visiting the community a part of my students' teaching-learning activity, then they will develop a sense of belonging and become less self-centred and more community-centred.

Another student penned this poem as part of her assignment documenting the changes in thinking that she is experiencing:

> Education that supports a web created with hand, heart, head and spirit
> Where learners acquire knowledge and DECIDE what to do with it
> Connective education that "enables all lives to flourish" . . .
> now and in the "different futures"
>
> . . . . . .
>
> Education that transcends space and allows the teacher to say:
> These are the possibilities, these are the approaches, what do YOU think is the best way to deal with "it"?
> Education that seeks to TRANSFORM!

These students, many of whom are currently working in the formal education system and some who are desirous of moving into non-formal education, represent a growing group of educators engaging in the self-reflective processes that underlie the transformative imperatives of ESD.

CONCLUSION

THE ISLAND AND MAINLAND NATIONS of the Caribbean region have specific geographical and socio-economic particularities and vulnerabilities that necessitate their pursuit of sustainable development – a paradigm that balances and harmonizes environmental sustainability, social inclusion, good governance and economic prosperity (Sachs 2015). For this to move from an ideal to a reality, however, ESD must be at its foundation to ensure that individuals, communities and nations understand sustainability, its associated issues and their interlinkages; develop values and attitudes that are consistent with sustainability principles, such as respect, tolerance, peace and care; develop skills that can support sustainability, such as critical-thinking, decision-making, problem-solving, reflective thinking, communication and collaborative skills; and translate all of this into behaviour change and action.

Within this text, we have outlined the concept of sustainable development, traced the historical development and evolution of the concept of ESD, and discussed the realities of the Caribbean that necessitate both sustainable development and ESD. We have underscored the importance of values and values education, and have argued for an underlying shift in our individual, societal and global value systems, as this is needed for sustainability to truly be sustained. We have also highlighted critical impediments to sustainable development in the region, such as climate change and violence, and what ESD-related educations, such as climate change education and peace education, should and must look like to engender mitigation behaviours and adaptive capacities, and peace-building within the region.

We also spoke to the importance of teacher education in developing the capacity of educators in the region to bring about the fundamental curricular, teaching and learning shifts needed within our education systems to support and institutionalize ESD. Importantly, we shared exemplars of ESD pedagogy, processes and practices grounded in and responsive to the Caribbean regional context.

Where do we go from here then? Drawing on Buckles (2018), two imperatives are necessary. First, we need to "recognize and act upon the foundational truth that all life upon Earth (including human beings) is dependent upon the living and non-living processes of the Earth" (Buckles 2018, viii). If we fail to recognize this as one of those pre-eminent truths, then we will continue on the current steady path of exploitation and destruction of not only our planet but of humanity. Second, each of us, along with our political, business and civil society leaders need to ask ourselves "a key ethical question, 'what kind of planet do we wish to pass on to our children and all living and non-living things?' " because it is only then that "we (that is humankind), can refocus how we live so that the planet that we live and depend upon can flourish" (Buckles 2018, viii).

Education can support both imperatives by fostering an understanding of that first pre-eminent truth and then by forcing us to reflect on the ethical question Buckles proposes and to take the necessary action to move us towards the kind of planet we envision. Indeed, in the Caribbean, education has begun the movement towards this path through, for instance, efforts to include sustainability content in school curricula, reorient teacher education towards sustainability and undertake non-formal education. There is, however, much more that needs to be done. We end, therefore, by proposing a few key recommendations as follows:

- Continued and sustained efforts to reorient education towards sustainability at all levels – pre-, primary, secondary and tertiary – and in both formal and non-formal modes, to ensure that ESD is part of the teaching and learning process of all ages, all levels of society and all sectors. A whole-institution approach to ESD should be encouraged to ensure reach and effectiveness.

- A concerted and sustained focus on teacher education, as a follow-on from the above recommendation and as outlined in chapter 4. This includes the infusion of ESD into curricula in certificate, diploma and degree programmes in regional teachers' colleges, universities and other institutions of higher education. Alongside this, there needs to be greater collaboration and partnering among (1) the teachers' colleges and the universities and (2) across the five campuses of the UWI. As previously articulated, the Caribbean Network of Teacher Educators and/or the MESCA network need to be revived as networks for capacity-building, resource creation and sharing, and professional development.

- Teaching, learning and assessment to move beyond education that is detached from individuals' realities and contexts, and beyond the assessment of knowledge and recall to teaching and learning that is grounded in context, responds to context and assesses students' capacities to think, reflect and act.

- Values clarification and reflection to be a central part of education in the region to ensure that individuals begin to interrogate the underlying values that have led to unsustainability (for example, consumerism) and the value changes that are needed in the transition to sustainability.

- Concerted and sustained focus on climate change and peace teaching and learning as integral aspects of ESD. These focal areas need to be incorporated into educational systems within the region at all levels given that climate change and violence are two of those issues that have great potential to impede sustainability within the region.

Of course, research needs to be an integral aspect of these various educational shifts to ensure practice that is evidence-based and grounded. Note, though, that this must be research that connects the university (students and lecturers) with the community, involves the community and feeds back into the community so that the formal and non-formal educational spheres are bridged.

To transform our world, we need a transformed people. We need a people who have learned to recognize the sacredness of all life. Education for sustainable development acknowledges this and so it is centred on developing students with deep care and respect for all of life. Students learn knowledge, skills and values that enable them to demonstrate this and so effect the changes needed for saving our planet. However, ESD itself needs to continue to evolve as it learns how to redefine and measure educational success in terms of the transformation that students have initiated in their various communities.

REFERENCES

Anderson, Jeffrey. 1999. "Service-Learning and Teacher Education". https://www
.ericdigests.org/1999-1/service.html.

Arisi, Regina O. 2013. "Culture and Moral Values for Sustainable National Development:
The Role of Social Studies Education". *International Review of Social Sciences and
Humanities* 5 (1): 247–54.

Assadourian, Erik. 2010. "The Rise and Fall of Consumer Cultures". In *2010 State of the
World: Transforming Cultures from Consumerism to Sustainability,* edited by Linda
Starke and Lisa Mastny, 3–20. Washington, DC: Worldwatch Institute.

Atkinson, Hugh. 2015. "Planetary Challenges: The Agenda Laid Bare". In *The Challenge
of Sustainability: Linking Politics, Education and Learning*, edited by Hugh Atkinson
and Ros Wade, 11–42. Bristol: Policy Press.

Bailey, Cathryn. 2009. "A Man and a Dog in a Lifeboat: Self-Sacrifice, Animals, and the
Limits of Ethical Theory". *Ethics and the Environment* 14 (1): 129–48.

Barker, David, David Dodman and Duncan McGregor. 2009. "Caribbean Vulnerability
and Global Change: Contemporary Perspectives". In *Global Change and Caribbean
Vulnerability: Environment, Economy and Society at Risk*, edited by Duncan
McGregor, David Dodman and David Barker, 3–21. Kingston: University of the
West Indies Press.

Benjamin, Lisa. 2010. "Climate Change and Caribbean Small Island Developing States:
The State of Play". *International Journal of Bahamian Studies* 16:78–91.

Billig, Shelley H, and Stephany Brown. 2009. "Service Learning to Enhance Academic
Achievement". https://vdocuments.net/service-learning-to-enhance-academic
-achievement-shelley-h-billig-stephany.html.

Boyne, Ian. 2012. "What's an Education For?" *Gleaner,* 7 October 2012. http://jamaica
-gleaner.com/gleaner/20121007/focus/focus1.html.

Bramwell-Lalor, Sharon. 2019. "Assessment for Learning on Sustainable Development".
In *Encyclopedia of Sustainability in Higher Education*, edited by Walter Leal Filho,
1–9. Cham, Switzerland: Springer. https://doi.org/10.1007/978-3-319-63951-2_1-1.

Brandt, Jan-Ole, Lina Burgener, Matthias Barth and Aaron Redman. 2019. "Becoming a Competent Teacher in Education for Sustainable Development: Learning Outcomes and Processes in Teacher Education". *International Journal of Sustainability in Higher Education* 20 (4): 630–53.

Buckles, Jeff. 2018. *Education, Sustainability and the Ecological Imaginary: Connective Education and Global Change*. Cham, Switzerland: Palgrave Macmillan.

Bynoe, Paulette. 2019. "Promoting Arts Based Environmental Education for Primary School Pupils in Guyana". *Eco-Thinking* 1 (1). https://journals.lib.sfu.ca/index.php/journal/index.

Bynoe, Paulette, and Denise Simmons. 2014. "An Appraisal of Climate Change Education at the Primary Level in Guyana". *Caribbean Geography* 19:89–103.

Cambers, Gillian. 2008. "Sandwatch: A Cross Disciplinary Approach to Education for Sustainable Development". In *Teachers' Guide for Education for Sustainable Development in the Caribbean*, edited by Ushio Miura, 77–97. Santiago: UNESCO.

Carby, Barbara, and Therese Ferguson. 2018. "An Exploratory Study of Disaster Risk Management Information for Persons with Disabilities in the Caribbean". *Caribbean Quarterly* 64 (1): 57–78.

Carless, David. 2017. "Students' Experiences of Assessment for Learning". In *Scaling up Assessment for Learning in Higher Education*, edited by David Carless, Susan M. Bridges, Cecilia Ka Yuk Chan and Rick Glofcheski, 113–26. Singapore: Springer..

Chevannes, Paulette. 2005. "Change from Within: A Model for Change in Jamaican Schools". *Caribbean Childhoods* 2:100–114.

Christodoulou, Eleni, Jorg Robert Schreiber, Yoko Mochizuki, Hannes E. Siege and Robert Stevenson. 2017. Introduction to *Textbooks for Sustainable Development: A Guide to Embedding*, edited by Maria Ainley-Taylor, 157–86. New Delhi: UNESCO MGIEP.

Coffin, Charles. 2001. *The Complete Poetry and Selected Prose of John Donne*. New York: Modern Library.

Cole, Sharline, and Susan Anderson. 2016. "Family Interaction and the Development of Aggression in Adolescents: The Experiences of Students and Administrators". *American International Journal of Contemporary Research* 6 (4): 12–21.

Collins-Figueroa, Marceline. 2012. "Biodiversity and Education for Sustainable Development in Teacher Education Programmes of Four Jamaican Educational Institutions". *Journal of Education for Sustainable Development* 6 (2): 253–67.

Collins-Figueroa, Marceline, Lorna Down, Carol Hordatt Gentles, Mariette Newman and Vileitha Davis-Morrison. 2011. "Concepts of Professionalism among Prospective Teachers in Jamaica". *Caribbean Journal of Education* 33 (2): 176–201.

Collins-Figueroa, Marceline, Gina Sanguinetti Phillips, Elaine Foster-Allen and Carlette Falloon. 2008. "Advancing Jamaican Formal Education through Environmental

Education for Sustainable Development". *Caribbean Journal of Education* 30 (1): 160–76.

Cooper, Carolyn. 2019. "Jamaican Bauxite Flies to the Moon". *Gleaner,* 3 November 2019. https://jamaica-gleaner.com/article/commentary/20191103/carolyn-cooper -jamaican-bauxite-flies-moon.

Crowell, Sam. 2017. *Earth Charter Pedagogy 2.0: New Understandings of Emergence Applied to ESD.* Kindle edition.

Davies, Lynn. 2006. "Global Citizenship: Abstraction or Framework for Action?" *Educational Review* 58 (1): 5–25.

Davis-Morrison, Vileitha, and Dian McCallum. 2003. "Educating for Values, Attitudes, and Character Development: Policy and Practice in the Formal Curriculum in Social Studies and History". *Caribbean Journal of Education* 25 (2): 103–28.

Delors, Jacques, In'am Al Mufti, Isao Amagi, Roberto Carneiro, Fay Chung, Bronislaw Geremek, William Gorham et al. 1996. *Learning: The Treasure Within: Report to UNESCO of the International Commission on Education for the Twenty-First Century.* Paris: UNESCO.

DeNobile, John, and Erin Hogan. 2014. "Values Education: What, How, Why and What Next?" *Curriculum and Leadership Journal* 12 (1). http://www.curriculum.edu.au /leader/volume_12_number_1,36843.html?issueID=12833.

Down, Keisha-Ann, and Lorna Down. 2018. "Implementers' Perspectives on Creating Successful Education for Sustainable Development Projects". *Caribbean Quarterly* 64 (1): 167–87.

Down, Lorna. 2003. "Literature: A Classroom Tool for Transformation and Sustainability". *Caribbean Journal of Education* 25 (2): 91–102.

———. 2005. "Literature to Address the Problem of Violence". In *Guidelines and Recommendations for Reorienting Teacher Education to Address Sustainability,* UNESCO, 18–19. Paris: UNESCO.

———. 2006. "Addressing the Challenges of Mainstreaming Education for Sustainable Development into Higher Education". *International Journal of Sustainability in Higher Education* 7 (4): 390–99.

———. 2007. "Literature to Address the Problem of Violence: Infusing ESD in the Curriculum". In *Good Practices in Education for Sustainable Development: Teacher Education Institutions,* edited by UNESCO, 7–10. Paris: UNESCO. https://unesdoc .unesco.org/ark:/48223/pf0000152452

———. 2008. "Infusing Education for Sustainable Development into the Teaching of Literature". In *Teachers' Guide for Education for Sustainable Development in the Caribbean,* edited by Ushio Miura, 37–51. Santiago: UNESCO.

———. 2010. "Teaching and Learning in, with and for Community: Towards a Pedagogy for Education for Sustainable Development". *Southern African Journal of Environmental Education* 27:58–70.

———. 2011. "Beginning Teachers as Change Agents for Sustainable Societies: Exploring the Relationship between Beginning Teachers' Concept of Change Agency and the Concept of Sustainability". *Caribbean Journal of Education* 33 (1): 39–60.

———. 2015a. "Engaging Mindfully with the Commons: A Case of Caribbean Teachers' Experience with ESD". *Applied Environmental Education and Communication* 15:105–11.

———. 2015b. "Transforming School Culture through Education for Sustainable Development (ESD)". *Journal of Eastern Caribbean Studies* 40 (3): 157–67.

———. 2019. "The Change from Within Programme: Creating a Culture of Peace in Schools through Social Affirmation". *Caribbean Journal of Education* 41 (2): 110–24.

Down, Lorna, and Thelma Baker. 2020. *Caribbean Writers on Teaching Literature*. Kingston: University of the West Indies Press.

Down, Lorna, Clement Lambert and Ceva McPherson-Kerr. 2005. *Violence in Schools and the Change from Within Project*. Kingston: Institute of Education.

Down, Lorna, Chintan Modi, Ivy Sek and sj Miller. 2017. "Language". In *Textbooks for Sustainable Development: A Guide to Embedding*, edited by Maria Ainley-Taylor, 157–86. New Delhi: UNESCO MGIEP.

Down, Lorna, and Henderson Nurse. 2007. "Education for Sustainable Development Networks, Potential and Challenge: A Critical Reflection on the Formation of the Caribbean Regional Network". *Journal of Education for Teaching* 33 (2): 177–90.

Earth Charter Commission. 1992. The Earth Charter. https://earthcharter.org/.

Edwards-Kerr, Deon. 2017. "Violence in Schools in Jamaica". In *Re-Imagining Education in the Commonwealth Caribbean*, edited by Zellynne Jennings and Deon-Edwards Kerr, 123–33. Kingston: Ian Randle.

ENACT (Environmental Action Programme). 2001. "ENACT and JBTE Facilitate Environmental Education in Teachers' Colleges". *Enviro Ed Link* 1 (1): 1, 4.

———. 2003. "Sustainable Teacher Environmental Education Project Augurs an Optimistic Future for Greening Teachers' Colleges". *Enviro Ed Link* 3 (1): 1.

Ernest, Paul. 2005. "Platform: Why Teach Mathematics?" *Mathematics in School* 34 (1): 28–29.

Exton, Mark, and Walter Enloe. 2014. "Lessons from Hiroshima: Building Cultures of Peace in International Education". *International Schools Journal* 34 (1): 20–26.

Ferguson, Therese. 2008a. "'Nature' and the 'Environment' in Jamaica's Primary School Curriculum Guides". *Environmental Education Research* 14 (5): 559–77.

———. 2008b. "Preservice Teachers' Views on Nature, the Environment and Sustainable Development: Implications for Teacher Education". *Caribbean Journal of Education* 30 (1): 108–35.

———. 2016. "School Violence and Sustainable Development: Change from Within". *Jamaica Observer*, 13 December 2016, 14.

———. 2017. "Shaping School Culture through Change from Within". *Jamaica Observer*, 22 August 2017, 14.

———. 2019a. "Addressing Anti-Social Behaviour and Violence as Barriers to Learning: Lessons from Jamaica's Change from Within Programme". In *Achieving Inclusive Education in the Caribbean and Beyond: From Philosophy to Praxis*, edited by Stacey Blackman, Dennis Conrad and Launcelot Brown, 133–44. Cham, Switzerland: Springer.

———. 2019b. "Climate Change Education for Sustainable Development". In *Encyclopedia of Sustainability in Higher Education*, edited by Walter Leal Filho. Cham, Switzerland: Springer.

———. 2019c. "Reflection, Dialogue, and Transformation through Participatory Action Research: Experiences of Jamaica's Change from Within Programme". In *Decolonizing Qualitative Approaches for and by the Caribbean*, edited by Saran Stewart, 139–58. Charlotte, NC: Information Age.

Ferguson, Therese, and Sharon Bramwell-Lalor. 2018. "Tertiary-Level Sustainability and Climate Change Education: Curricula Development Efforts for Caribbean Teachers". *Caribbean Quarterly* 64 (1): 79–99.

Ferguson, Therese, and Paulette Chevannes. 2018. "The Change from Within Program: Bringing Restorative Justice Circles for Conflict Resolution to Jamaican Schools". *Childhood Education: Innovations* 94 (1): 55–61.

Ferguson, Therese, Tenesha Gordon, Shaughna-Lee Steele and Dena Rae Samuels. 2020. "Changing School Cultures from Within". *Social and Economic Studies* 69 (1–2): 165–88.

Ferguson, Therese, Dena Rae Samuels and Tenesha Gordon. 2018. "More than Therapeutic: The Role of the Change from Within Programme's 'Circle of Friends' in Leadership Development to Address Violence". *Journal of Education and Development in the Caribbean* 17 (2): 1–30.

Ferreira, C., and Salome Schulze. 2014. "Teachers' Experience of the Implementation of Values in Education in Schools: 'Mind the Gap'". *South African Journal of Education* 34 (1). http://www.sajournalofeducation.co.za/index.php/saje.

Ferreira, Jo-Anne, Lisa Ryan and Daniella Tilbury. 2007. "Mainstreaming Education for Sustainable Development in Initial Teacher Education in Australia: A Review of Existing Professional Development Models". *Journal of Education for Teaching* 33 (2): 225–39.

Fullan, Michael. 2002. "Moral Purpose Writ Large". *School Administrator* (online edition). https://michaelfullan.ca/wp-content/uploads/2016/06/13396048660.pdf.

————, ed. 2009. *The Challenge of Change: Start School Improvement Now!* Thousand Oaks, CA: Corwin.

Garrard, Greg. 2007. "Ecocriticism and Education for Sustainability". *Pedagogy: Critical Approaches to Teaching Literature, Language, Composition, and Culture* 7 (3): 359–83.

Gentle-Genitty, Carolyn, Jangmin Kim, Eun-Hye Yi, Douglas Slater, Beverly Reynolds and Natasha Bragg. 2017. "Comprehensive Assessment of Youth Violence in Five Caribbean Countries: Gender and Age Differences". *Journal of Human Behavior in the Social Environment* 27 (7): 745–59.

Gibb, Natalie. 2016. *Getting Climate-Ready: A Guide for Schools on Climate Action.* Paris: UNESCO. https://unesdoc.unesco.org/ark:/48223/pf0000246740.

Griffith, Stafford. 2015. *School-Based Assessment in a Caribbean Public Examination.* Kingston: University of the West Indies Press.

Guo, Linyuan. 2014. "Preparing Teachers to Educate for 21st Century Global Citizenship: Envisioning and Enacting". *Journal of Global Citizenship and Equity Education* 4 (1): 1–23.

Harris, Ian, and Mary Lee Morrison. 2013. *Peace Education.* Jefferson, NC: McFarland.

Hendrickson, Dean. 1974. "Why Do We Teach Mathematics?" *Mathematics Teacher* 67 (5): 468–70.

Heyneman, Stephen. 2009. "The Importance of External Examinations in Education". In *Secondary School External Examination Systems: Reliability, Robustness and Resilience*, edited by Barend Vlaardingerbroek and Neil Taylor, 1–11. New York: Cambria Press.

Hordatt Gentles, Carol. 2018. "Reorienting Jamaican Teacher Education to Address Sustainability". *Caribbean Quarterly* 64 (1): 149–66.

Inman, Sally, Sophie Mackay, Maggie Rogers and Ros Wade. 2010. "Effecting Change through Learning Networks: The Experience of the UK Teacher Education Network for Education for Sustainable Development and Global Citizenship". *Journal of Teacher Education for Sustainability* 12 (2): 97–109.

IPCC (Intergovernmental Panel on Climate Change). 2014. *Climate Change 2014: Synthesis Report. Contribution of Working Groups I, II and III to the Fifth Assessment Report of the Intergovernmental Panel on Climate Change.* Geneva: IPCC.

Johnston, Ronald A., Anita Rampal, Annie Hale, Julito Aligaen and Mijung Kim. 2017. "Science". In *Textbooks for Sustainable Development: A Guide to Embedding*, edited by Maria Ainley-Taylor, 67–100. New Delhi: UNESCO MGIEP.

Kapucu, Naim, and Alpaslan Ozerdem. 2013. *Managing Emergencies and Crises.* Burlington, MA: Jones and Bartlett Learning.

Kaye, Cathryn. 2004. *The Complete Guide to Service Learning: Proven, Practical Ways to Engage Students in Civic Responsibility, Academic Curriculum, and Social Action.* Minneapolis: Free Spirit.

Kimmerer, Robin Wall. 2013. *Braiding Sweetgrass: Indigenous Wisdom, Scientific Knowledge and the Teaching of Plants*. Minneapolis: Milkweed Editions.

Knight, Verna. 2015. "Disaster Risk Reduction Education in the Caribbean: Policy, Practice, and Implications for Teacher Education". *Journal of Eastern Caribbean Studies* 40 (3): 187–209.

Kopnina, Helen. 2014. "Education for Sustainable Development (ESD): Exploring Anthropocentric-Ecocentric Values in Children through Vignettes". *Studies in Educational Evaluation* 41:124–32.

Kostoulas-Makrakis, Nelly. 2010. "Developing and Applying a Critical and Transformative Model to Address Education for Sustainable Development in Teacher Education". *Journal of Teacher Education for Sustainability* 12 (2): 17–26.

Larson-Keagy, Elizabeth. 2015. "Civic Responsibility and Service Learning: The Need for Curricular Integration". https://www.mesacc.edu/community-civic-engagement/journals/civic-responsibility-and-service-learning-need-curricular.

Laurie, Robert, Yuko Nonoyama-Tarumi, Rosalyn McKeown and Charles Hopkins. 2016. "Contributions of Education for Sustainable Development (ESD) to Quality Education: A Synthesis of Research". *Journal of Education for Sustainable Development* 10 (2): 226–42.

Lausselet, Nadia Sangita, Glenn William Chickering, Stefano Malatesta and Yemuna Sunny. 2017. "Geography". In *Textbooks for Sustainable Development: A Guide to Embedding*, edited by Maria Ainley-Taylor, 103–53. New Delhi: UNESCO MGIEP.

Leicht, Alexander, Julia Heiss and Won Jung Byun, eds. 2018. *Issues and Trends in Education for Sustainable Development*. Paris: UNESCO.

Lotz-Sisitka, Heila, Arjen E J Wals, David Kronlid and Dylan McGarry. 2015. "Transformative, Transgressive Social Learning: Rethinking Higher Education Pedagogy in Times of Systemic Global Dysfunction". *Current Opinion in Environmental Sustainability* 16:73–80.

Lovat, Terence, and Neville Clement. 2008. "The Pedagogical Imperative of Values Education". *Journal of Beliefs and Values* 29 (3): 273–85.

Lovelace, Earl. 1979. *The Dragon Can't Dance*. London: Andre Deutsch.

McDougall, Christine. 2021. "Inquiry and Participatory Action Research in Primary School". *Caribbean Journal of Education* 42 (1–2): 157–205.

McGregor, Duncan, David Dodman and David Barker, eds. 2009. *Global Change and Caribbean Vulnerability: Environment, Economy and Society at Risk*. Kingston: University of the West Indies Press.

McKeown, Rosalyn. 2014. "The Leading Edge of Teacher Education and ESD". *Journal of Education for Sustainable Development* 8 (2): 127–31.

Meeks, Brian. 2005. *Envisioning Caribbean Futures: Jamaican Perspectives*. Kingston: University of the West Indies Press.

Miller, Errol. 2003. *The Prophet and the Virgin: The Masculine and Feminine Roots of Teaching*. Kingston: Ian Randle.

Ministry of Education. Jamaica. 2009. *Health and Family Life Education Teacher Training Manual*. Kingston: Ministry of Education.

———. 2012. *National Education Strategic Plan: 2011–2020*. Kingston: Ministry of Education.

Morris, Mervyn. 1992. *Examination Centre*. London: New Beacon Books.

Noddings, Nel. 2002. *Educating Moral People: A Caring Alternative to Character Education*. New York: Teachers College Press.

Nolet, Victor. 2016. *Educating for Sustainability: Principles and Practices for Teachers*. New York: Routledge.

Novacek, Pavel. 2013. "Human Values Compatible with Sustainable Development". *Journal of Human Values* 19 (1): 5–13.

Orr, David. 1992. *Ecological Literacy, Education and the Transition to a Postmodern World*. New York: SUNY Press.

Oxfam. 2015. *Global Citizenship in the Classroom: A Guide for Teachers*. Oxford: Oxfam.

Peters, Michael, Alan Britton and Harry Blee. 2008. "Introduction: Many Faces of Global Civil Society: Possible Futures for Global Citizenship". In *Global Citizenship Education: Philosophy, Theory and Pedagogy*, edited by Michael Peters, Alan Britton and Harry Blee, 1–13. Rotterdam: Sense.

PIOJ (Planning Institute of Jamaica). 2009. *Vision 2030 Jamaica: National Development Plan*. Kingston: PIOJ.

Ramphall, David. 1997. "Postmodernism and the Rewriting of Caribbean Radical Development Thinking". *Social and Economic Studies* 46 (1): 1–30.

Rhiney, Kevon. 2015. "Geographies of Caribbean Vulnerability in a Changing Climate: Issues and Trends". *Geography Compass* 9 (3): 97–114.

Rieckmann, Marco. 2018. "Learning to Transform the World: Key Competencies in Education for Sustainable Development". In *Issues and Trends in Education for Sustainable Development*, edited by Alexander Leicht, Julia Heiss and Won Jung Byun, 39–59. Paris: UNESCO.

Rockström, Johan, Will Steffen, Kevin Noone, Åsa Persson, F. Stuart III Chapin, Eric Lambin, Timothy M. Lenton et al. 2009. "Planetary Boundaries: Exploring the Safe Operating Space for Humanity". *Ecology and Society* 14 (2): 32. http://www.ecologyandsociety.org/vol14/iss2/art32/.

Rohr, Richard. 2019. "The Great Turning". https://cac.org/the-great-turning-2019-11-04/.

Roofe, Carmel, and Therese Ferguson. 2018. "Technical and Vocational Education and Training Curricular Subjects at the Lower Secondary Level in Jamaica: A Preliminary Exploration of Education for Sustainable Development Content". *Discourse and Communication for Sustainable Education* 9 (2): 93–110.

Roofe, Carmel, Therese Ferguson, Carol Hordatt Gentles, Sharon Bramwell-Lalor, Loraine Cook, Aldrin E. Sweeney, Canute Thompson and Everton Cummings. 2021. "Infusing Education for Sustainable Development into Curricula: Teacher Educators' Experiences within the School of Education at the University of the West Indies, Jamaica". In *Teaching and Sustainable Development: Using the Transformative Power of Teaching to Raise Awareness on Sustainable Development and Achieve the UN Sustainable Development Goals*, edited by Walter Leal Filho, Amanda Salvia and Fernanda Frankenberger, 133–51. Cheltenham: Edward Elgar.

Sachs, Jeffrey. 2015. *The Age of Sustainable Development*. New York: Columbia University Press.

Santone, Susan. 2019. "Reclaiming Education as a Public Good: Place-Based Teacher Education". *Childhood Education* 95 (5): 66–69.

Schumacher, Ernest. 1990. *Small Is Beautiful: A Study of Economics as if People Mattered*. Vancouver: Harper and Marks.

Sen, Amartya. 1999. *Development as Freedom*. New York: Anchor Books.

Senah, Emmanuel K. 2006. *Core Curriculum Guide for Strengthening Morals and Values Education in Educational Institutions in Trinidad and Tobago*. Port-of-Spain: Ministry of Education.

Shallcross, Tony, and John Robinson. 2007. "Is a Decade of Teacher Education for Sustainable Development Essential for Survival?" *Journal of Education for Teaching* 33 (2): 127–47.

Sinek, Simon. 2009. "How Great Leaders Inspire Action". Filmed in Puget Sound, WA, September 2009. TEDxPuget Sound video, 17:48. https://www.ted.com/talks /simon_sinek_how_great_leaders_inspire_action.

Spiller, Dorothy. 2012. "Assessment Matters: Self-Assessment and Peer Assessment". http://cei.ust.hk/files/public/assessment_matters_self-assessment_peer_assessment .pdf.

Stephenson, Kimberly, Michael A. Taylor, Tannecia S. Stephenson, Abel Centella, Arnoldo Bezanilla and John Charlerly. 2018. "The Regional Climate Science Initiative: Value Added and Lessons Learnt". *Caribbean Quarterly* 64 (1): 11–25.

Sterling, Stephen. 2010. "What Is Learning for Sustainable Development?" In *Tomorrow Today*, edited by Michele Witthaus, Karen McCandless and Rebecca Lambert, 32–33. Leicester, UK: Tudor Rose.

Stiggins, Rick. 2005. "From Formative Assessment to Assessment for Learning: A Path to Success in Standards-Based Schools". *Phi Delta Kappan* 87 (4): 324–28.

Stone, Rosemarie, ed. 1995. *Carl Stone Speaks on People, Politics and Development*. Kingston: n.p.

Sumara, Dennis. 2002. *Why Reading Literature in School Still Matters*. Mahwah, NJ: Lawrence Erlbaum.

Sutton, Heather, Laura Jaitman and Jeetendra Khadan. 2017. "Violence in the Caribbean: Cost and Impact". In *Unleashing Growth and Strengthening Resilience in the Caribbean*, edited by Trevor Alleyne, Inci Otker, Uma Ramakrishnan and Krishna Srinivasan, 329–45. Washington, DC: International Monetary Fund.

Sutton, Heather, and Inder Ruprah. 2017. "Introduction: Combatting Crime and Restoring Paradise". In *Restoring Paradise in the Caribbean: Combatting Violence with Numbers*, edited by Heather Sutton and Inder Ruprah, ix–xii. Washington, DC: Inter-American Development Bank.

Tamarack Media Corporation. 2020. "Do We Need to Rethink Our Ideas of Time?" https://www.bbc.co.uk/ideas/videos/do-we-need-to-re-think-our-ideas-of-time/po818lnv?playlist=sustainable-thinking.

Taylor, Michael. 2015. *Why Climate Demands Change*. GraceKennedy Lecture. Kingston: GraceKennedy Foundation. http://gracekennedy.com/lecture/GKL2015-Climate.pdf.

———. 2019. "Climate Basics: The What? Why? And How?" [PowerPoint slides].

Taylor, Michael, Tannecia Stephenson, Anthony Chen and Kimberly Stephenson. 2012. "Climate Change and the Caribbean: Review and Response". *Caribbean Studies* 40 (2): 169–200.

Thomas-Hope, Elizabeth. 1996. *The Environmental Dilemma in Caribbean Context*. Grace Kennedy Lecture. Kingston: Grace Kennedy Foundation.

UNCED (United Nations Conference on Environment and Development). 1992. *Agenda 21: Programme of Action for Sustainable Development*. New York: UN. https://sustainabledevelopment.un.org/content/documents/Agenda21.pdf.

UNDP (United Nations Development Programme). 2012. *Caribbean Human Development Report 2012: Human Development and the Shift to Better Citizen Security*. New York: UNDP.

UNDP (United Nations Development Programme). 2020. *Human Development Report 2020: The Next Frontier: Human Development and the Anthropocene*. New York: UNDP. http://hdr.undp.org/en/content/human-development-report-2020.

UNECE (United Nations Economic Commission for Europe). 2012. *Learning for the Future: Competences in Education for Sustainable Development*. Geneva: UNECE.

UNESCO (United Nations Educational, Scientific and Cultural Organization). 2005. *United Nations Decade of Education for Sustainable Development 2005–2014: Draft International Implementation Scheme*. Paris: UNESCO.

———. 2006. *Framework for the UNDESD International Implementation Scheme*. Paris: UNESCO.

———. 2010. *Sandwatch: Adapting to Climate Change and Educating for Sustainable Development*. Paris: UNESCO.

———. 2012. *Education for Sustainable Development Sourcebook*. Paris: UNESCO.

————. 2014. *UNESCO Roadmap for Implementing the Global Action Programme on Education for Sustainable Development*. Paris: UNESCO.

————. 2015. *Global Citizenship Education: Topics and Learning Objectives*. Paris: UNESCO.

————. 2020. "What Is Education for Sustainable Development?" https://en.unesco.org /themes/education-sustainable-development/what-is-esd.

————. 2021. "Berlin Declaration on Education for Sustainable Development". https:// en.unesco.org/sites/default/files/esdfor2030-berlin-declaration-en.pdf.

UNICEF (United Nations Children's Fund). 1999. *Peace Education in UNICEF*. New York: UNICEF.

————. 2009. *Towards a Learning Culture of Safety and Resilience: Technical Guidance for Integrating Disaster Risk Reduction in the School Curriculum*. Geneva and Paris: UNICEF/UNESCO.

UNITWIN/UNESCO Chair on Reorienting Teacher Education to Address Sustainability and the International Network of Teacher Education Institutions (INTEI). 2005. *Guidelines and Recommendations for Reorienting Teacher Education to Address Sustainability*. Paris: UNESCO.

UWI (University of the West Indies). 2017. *The UWI Triple A Strategy 2017–2022: Revitalizing Caribbean Development*. Kingston: UWI. https://www.mona.uwi .edu/principal/departments/opair/uwi-strategic-plan.

UWI and UNEP (University of the West Indies and the United Nations Environment Programme). 2011. *Report of the Audit: Mainstreaming Environment and Sustainability in Caribbean Universities (MESCA)*. Kingston: UWI and UNEP.

Wagner, David Richard, Antonious Franz Warmeling, Masami Isoda and Parvin Sinclair. 2017. "Mathematics". In *Textbooks for Sustainable Development: A Guide to Embedding*, edited by Maria Ainley-Taylor, 35–63. New Delhi: UNESCO MGIEP.

Wahyudin, Dinn. 2018. "Peace Education in the Context of Education Sustainable Development". *Journal of Sustainable Development Education and Research* 2 (1): 21–32.

WCED (World Commission on Environment and Development). 1987. *Our Common Future*. Oxford: Oxford University Press.

Whitman, Cheryl Vince. 2004. "Uniting Three Initiatives on Behalf of Caribbean Youth and Educators: Health and Family Life Education and the Health Promoting School in the Context of PANCAP's Strategic Framework for HIV/AIDS". *Caribbean Quarterly* 50 (1): 54–82.

Williams, Hakim Mohanda Amani. 2017. "Teachers' Nascent Praxes of Care: Potentially Decolonizing Approaches to School Violence in Trinidad". *Journal of Peace Education* 14 (1): 69–91.

Wilmot, Swithin. 2002. "A Stake in the Soil: Land and Creole Politics in Free Jamaica, the 1849 Elections". In *In the Shadow of the Plantation: Caribbean History and Legacy*, edited by Alvin O. Thompson, 314–30. Kingston: Ian Randle.

Wiltshire, Winthrop. 2008. "Empowering Teachers with Emotional Coping Skills to Promote Sustainable Development". In *Teachers' Guide for Education for Sustainable Development in the Caribbean*, edited by Ushio Miura, 11–19. Santiago: UNESCO.

INDEX

Note: *Italic* page numbers refer to figures and tables.